Cycling After Thomas

And The English

To

Sarah

In appreciation of your
support

David Caddy

David Caddy

Also by David Caddy

Poetry

The Balance (1981)
Anger (1982)
The Beating on the Door (1987)
Honesty (1990)
Continuity (1995)
Desire (1997)
The Willy Poems (2004)
Man in Black (2007)
The Bunny Poems (2011)

Literature

London: City of Words (with Westrow Cooper, 2006)

Criticism

So Here We Are (2012)

Cycling After Thomas

And The English

David Caddy

Spout Hill Press

First U.S. Edition
March 2013
Copyright ©2013 by David Caddy

For information about permissions to reproduce selections
from this book, contact Spout Hill Press at
spouthillpress@aol.com

www.spouthillpress.com
Walnut, California

Cover design by Ann Brantingham

ISBN 13: 978-0615779478
ISBN 10: 0615779476

To Chris Sargent, publican and Englishman

To Leon Dodson, Jed Drake and in memory of Paul Hart

Acknowledgements

An extract from Chapter Nine previously appeared in *Tears in the Fence* 56

My thanks go to Ann Brantingham for her patience and understanding in overseeing this publication. I thank Ann and John Brantingham for their encouragement at the beginning and Ann for her cover design.

I thank Ian Brinton for his Foreword and our conversations about Edward Thomas and *In Pursuit of Spring*. Ian has steered me away from making a fool of myself by his advice and considerable knowledge of Edward Thomas.

Thanks go to John Brantingham, Sarah Connor and Dave Newman for writing the cover blurbs.

Thank you Sarah Connor, Jed Drake and Dr. Rosie Jackson for our discussions on the divided brain within Western Culture and for your enthusiasm. I thank Dr. Mike Kearney for introducing me to The Imagined Village and Jethro Lyne for our discussions on English folk music.

Thanks go to Leon Dodson, Jed Drake, Marie Fisher, Adrian Fisher, Dr. Brian Hinton M.B.E. and Chris Sargent for our discussions on Englishness.

I have greatly benefitted from many conversations with Chris Sargent about the anthropology of the English pub. I also benefitted from the studies of Kate Fox.

Thanks also go to Leon Dodson and Rob Whittaker for their parts in this book.

My thanks go to Louise Anne Buchler for her comments on early drafts and for her inspiration. My faults are all mine.

Foreword

The passion Edward Thomas felt for walking and for the roads and paths which act as an intricate network crossing and re-crossing the south of England can be detected from his earliest writing. In a letter sent to Helen Noble in June 1897 he commented upon how he walked 'slowly and with downward eyes, almost without a thought' and in his first published book, *The Woodland Life*, he presented the reader with the mystery of paths that connect the world of the forest with that of the open country:

> When the path takes us out of the wood, we leave the sheltered stillness behind, and feel the cool breath of the breeze that has sprung up with the lifting of the fog. In the foliage of the oaks, still dense and shadowy, three wrens are singing in broken snatches.

The sense of mystery which haunts this early description, the sheltered world of the wood with its density and shadows, is one of the fascinations that paths held for Thomas and is one of the guiding threads that pulls David Caddy along the paths from London to his own sense of home. For the Thomas of *The Icknield Way* a path that seemed to have no beginning or end was the focus of his attention and it became for him 'a symbol of mortal things with their beginnings and ends always in immortal darkness.'

David talks of the poetry which Thomas wrote towards the end of his life, after the outbreak of the First World War, as re-enacting 'an absent presence in the form of a distance between the self and a dark place in free fall', a 'dislocation and state of collapse' which 'can only be filled by making a journey to the locality or by other restorative actions'. Thomas's poem 'The Path' was written in March 1915 and in it he recalled the way that his elder children used to walk and run down Old Stoner Hill near Steep in order to go to Bedales junior school. The opening lines immediately convey an exciting hint of danger in this pathway:

> Running along a bank, a parapet
> That saves from the precipitous wood below
> The level road, there is a path.

Not only is there a hint of the background of war with 'parapet' but the placing of 'precipitous' with its four syllables surrounded by simple monosyllables almost brings the reader to the edge, only to discover that at the end of the sentence 'there is a path.'

In D.H. Lawrence's *The Rainbow* two of the chapter headings are given as 'The Widening Circle' and the reference is both to expanding experience and the effects of the bicycle: a new world being opened up to the adventurer through the lanes of England. David's book re-enacts not only Thomas's pursuit of Spring but also a widening of experience in which we are allowed to see who we are against a background of heritage that is still there lurking up the bye-ways. One of Thomas's posthumously published essays took as its subject 'The First Cuckoo' and his language of nostalgic atmosphere and exact placing seems absolutely appropriate for this delightful book of David's own travels:

The road was deep in dust, but the marigolds in the ditch preserved their brightness and their coolness. Coming over the shoulder of the hill called Pwll y Pridd, by the farm Morfa Bach, where the primroses were so thick under the young emerald larches, I began to have a strong desire—almost amounting to a conviction—that I should hear the cuckoo.

—Ian Brinton

Chapter One

The Bicycle

One day I was at my desk thinking about cultural forgetfulness, how our collective memory seems to have shortened and yet the English have a deep love of history. I opened my copy of *In Pursuit of Spring* and began reading slowly. A quest to emulate Edward Thomas' cycle journey a century ago soon emerged and I was filled with excitement at the prospect.

There is a compelling mixture of mania and elegance in the writing and a sense of history through topography permeating identity. The book is peculiarly English and distinctly odd like a hand reaching out in the dark. It is a work of Modernism, more akin to a Picasso painting than a Turner, and not the work of a staid Georgian poet or hack journalist. It is the work of possessed man. I knew comparatively little about Thomas yet quickly realized his appropriation by critics, as a Georgian poet was not helpful. There is a slavish fashion amongst critics to follow each other in their approach and to put poets and writers into unsuitable groupings or boxes. I prefer to read closely, situating writers within their own historical-cultural connections and to ask different questions following where the answers lead. It is a matter of exacting contextualization and attention to detail in its own time.

Thomas chose to cycle rather than walk. The bicycle has a deep association with freedom and perspective. Raymond Queneau's last novel *Le vol d'Icare (The Flight of Icarus)* 1968 sees Icarus finding autonomy through a bicycle. Graham Robb's brilliant and award winning book, *The Discovery of France*, on the cultural and social history of France was researched on bicycle to help him imbibe a sense of France as much bigger and more varied than travelling by motor car or train would suggest. This worked as the book has a deep sense of local and regional diversity and historical perspective. Robb calculated that his bicycle would travel at the same rate as a nineteenth century stagecoach.

This was surely part of the reason that Thomas chose to cycle. His cycling suggests some urgency and carries with its choice some clear associations. The bicycle, inextricably linked with the New Woman and the Suffragette Movement, gave women unprecedented mobility. In the 1890s women defied convention and found independence from domestic and submissive roles. They discarded the restrictive clothing of the late-Victorian era in favour of more practical baggy trousers and skirts and cycled to work outside of the home. Suffragettes were invariably portrayed with their wheels. Kate Chopin's short stories bring out this altered perception of femininity and links the bicycle with her characters emotional and erotic needs. She would have been inspired by women such as Annie Kopchovsky, the Boston mother who cycled around the world in fifteen months for a wager. Re-inventing herself as Annie Londonderry, she gave up her role as a wife and mother to find freedom on a bicycle. In 1913 Suffragettes on bicycles carry a clear social message and signal a concern for increased democracy and human progress. Cycling is thus a symbolic act linked to social change.

I cycle to work and see the bicycle as a low-cost energy efficient, healthy means of transport. Bicycles are becoming lighter and faster with improved technology. A reasonably fit cyclist on a racing bicycle can quite easily reach speeds of 25-30 mph on flat surfaces. A sprightly octogenarian and life-long cyclist, who occasionally cycles with me for a chat before saying goodbye and disappearing out of view, baffled me until I discovered the virtue of his advanced bicycle. Taking a test run on a top of the range bicycle from your local bike shop is to be recommended but do not leave your glasses in the shop as I did. After one of the scariest experiences of my life I required a sit down and calming drink. Cycling is a means to freedom and of seeing the world. I have loved the feel of cycling and sense of freedom since I got the hang of staying upright on my 1950s Humber aged ten. When I graduated to a three gear Raleigh Sprite I had a sense of greater speed but less sturdiness. Those old solid bicycles, the BSAs, Humber, Triumph and Raleigh, were built to last. Nowadays I change my bicycle, a Trek or Giant, every three years. I think my old Humber lasted twenty years. In the summer of 1975, my then girlfriend and I bought new bicycles from Halfords in the Old Kent Road, London and discovered the joys and culture of Holland. Like D.H. Lawrence's self-portrait, Paul Morel, in *Sons and Lovers*, I too cycled under a spell to meet a lover and I have an ambition to cycle to my new love and present her with a red rose and an electric kiss. These are rites of passage.

Cycling is now more popular than it was in the Twenties and we are in the fourth cycling boom. Cycling is being advocated successfully as an alternative means of transport and there is a corollary movement encouraging the creation of conditions for improved utility and recreational cycling. According to a 2011 London School of Economics study, the 'Gross Cycling Product,' 3.7 million bicycles were sold in the UK in 2010, a 28% increase on 2009 and there were 1.3 million more cyclists than in the previous year. The report projects a 20% increase by 2015 with an increased contribution to the economy and annual savings in health benefits totaling £128 million and further savings in reduced traffic congestion and lower pollution levels. Further and regular cycling could increase the socio-economic benefits to the country considerably. Cycling and its accessories contributed £2.9 billion gross to the national economy in 2010 and that figure is rising annually. There are more cyclists seeking places to cycle and risking their lives on overcrowded streets and roads than ever before. One feels invigorated after a ride in much the same way as after a good walk, although that feeling is tempered by the antics of some drivers and the complete absence of safe cycling. As I cycle back from work at night, my problems come in the form of frightened badgers and deer and speeding motorists. Although organisations, such as Sustrans, are actively encouraging interest in a sustainable transport policy and *The Times* newspaper has a Cities Fit for Cycling campaign, cycling and cycle ways do not often feature in national or local transport policy. In fact, the proportion of GDP spent on public cycling infrastructure by the UK Government is lower than many other European countries. On the bright side, the National Cycle network has recently grown by 12,000 miles and is continuing to expand. The Common Transport Select Committee called on the Government to support Cities Fit For Cycling in July 2012 and to tackle the increasing death toll of cyclists on roads.

There are signs that the streets of some cities might be closed to cars in the near future. The popularity of cycling has been buoyed by Bradley Wiggins winning the Tour de France and our successes at the Olympic Games.

The Mayor of London, Boris Johnson, like his cycling predecessor, Ken Livingstone, certainly puts the motorist first in the tricky area of road space in London. He is though to be congratulated for advocating a 'cycling' revolution and introducing the Barclays Cycle Hire scheme, more cycle lanes and parking spaces in London. 22,000 people daily share 5,000 hire bikes thanks to the Barclays scheme. Despite problems it is undoubtedly a step forward. Demand for cycle ways, increased railway services and the restoration of lines and services cut following the 1963 Beeching Report, is growing but the motorist and the oil industry still dominate policy. Environmentally friendly alternatives and the concept of environmental value are given lip service rather than being openly embraced. The Beeching Cuts removed more than 4,000 miles of track and some 3,000 stations. This twin interest in the bicycle and train seems to be growing in direct proportion to the continual rise in oil costs and the realisation that alternatives to motor vehicles will need to be developed. The fuel crisis at the end of March 2012 when the Government advised people to stock up before a possible tanker driver strike, which never happened, highlighted the fragility of an economy over-dependent upon petrol and road transport. Locally there were ugly and violent scenes as motorists clambered for limited supplies. The loss of local garages exacerbated the situation and people began panic buying at supermarkets fearing a haulage driver strike.

As a child at Fiddleford I used to tell the time by the trains
and looked forward to the drivers tooting their whistle or
waving as they steamed past. The much faster Pines Express
with its long line of carriages en route to Manchester was a
memorable sight. The Somerset & Dorset Railway, or Slow &
Dirty, as it was nicknamed, joined the London Waterloo to
Exeter line at Templecombe and it was from there that the
Blackmore Vale had access to the wider world. At the age of
fifteen I would travel from Gillingham to Andover by steam
train to stay overnight with the Barnett family in order to run
for Andover Athletic Club on Saturday afternoon. There is
something deeply romantic about steam trains. This has been
utilised by David Lean in films, such as *Brief Encounter* and
Doctor Zhivago and more erotically in Jiri Menzel's *Closely
Observed Trains*. Menzel's film, set in a remote train station in
German occupied Czechoslovakia, connects local people to
events and actions in the wider world and magnifies the small
detail of local life in tender and funny ways. Its juxtaposition
of quirky eroticism, disarming comedy and tragedy make it
memorable. I read the film as a call for local independence
and it shows that trains have a double-edged role in that.
They connect the local to the national and beyond and back
again. It is a blast against stultifying bureaucracy in the guise
of a film about growing up. Heavily symbolic with sexual
imagery and voyeurism, it disturbs in its implication that the
local needs to become more independent as well as showing
that it is connected to wider things that it cannot control
without a resistance movement. The sexual growing up of the
shy young clerk, Milos, obsessed with the pretty train
conductor and losing his virginity is balanced with the
urgency and significance of each passing train. One

memorable scene involves Milos observing a randy station guard methodically rubber-stamping the naked bum of a peasant girl. The comedy makes this viewer want to break out and have fun, to be a local grown up, and I think that may be the point of this Oscar winning film.

The old S & D, which ran from Bournemouth to Bath, was closed in March 1966. I travelled, on one of the last trains to and from Poole, with my Mum and brother, and every carriage was overflowing. Surveyed on a Wednesday when shops closed was guaranteed to produce a negative picture of the line's economic future. Local protests went unheard. The removal of the steel railway bridges closed off links between towns and villages. Locals grumbled for decades and nothing was done. Since then the local population has more than trebled and heavily congested roads have become full of potholes and dangerous to travel upon. More than 95% of the original track bed survives and like a phoenix from the ashes, it is becoming alive again. I became passionate about the need for a Trailway and railway linking local villages and towns a few years ago. I see it as a sign of English vision and part of a counter to the corrupt and unethical business practices of Tesco supermarket and the loss of our local produce market and agriculture. Sturminster Newton, where I went to school, was once the site of Europe's biggest livestock market. The Trailway from Sturminster to Fiddleford opened in 2008 and has been extended to Shillingstone, Stourpaine and is due to reach Blandford this year. The entire line is gradually being opened for cyclists, horse riders, runners, dog walkers and walkers and rail restoration groups have begun to spring up at Shillingstone

and Spetisbury. I cycled the cracked road from Durweston to
Shillingstone Railway Station on Easter Day 2012 filled with
the joy of spring sunshine. Fields of oil seed rape and
celandines glistened on both sides of the road. My mind
drifted back to when I lived at Shillingstone and cycled to
work at the Sturminster creamery to make cheese the
traditional way and of drinking with Martin Drake, Lucy, Sara
and Jo Dove at either The Seymour Arms, now long gone,
and The Ox Inn, now a free house and making a comeback
as a result of its proximity to the Trailway. A buzzard flew
overhead as I approached Gains Cross. At the Station there
was a buzz of activity with people taking pictures on their
phones. There was an Easter Egg Hunt and families were
already in eager pursuit. I spoke to Derek, resplendent in
Station Guard uniform and hat, about acquiring leaflets, maps
and display materials for my local pub, The White Horse,
Stourpaine. Derek had been managing the shop and café for
two months and commuted from Fareham, sixty miles away,
every weekend to volunteer. The Station Project Chairman,
Squadron Leader, Toby Watkins, regularly motorbikes from
Lincolnshire to the Station. The bulk of the active
membership is relatively local and youngish, supported by
local haulage, hire and construction companies run by people
that I know. I have fond memories of enjoying a bottle or
three of quince and blackberry and apple wine with the
Antells, at the Great Dorset Steam Fair in 1989, as they
displayed their heavy haulage prowess until the early hours of
the morning, a succession of can-can girls dancing furiously
as they steamed by. The Station has been restored to its glory
days, with track laid towards Gains Cross and more to follow
and the development of an engineering works to restore the

engines and carriages that they have acquired. Since 2009 other projects to restore lost links along the S & D line have emerged at Midford, Midsomer Norton, Henstridge and Spetisbury. There is even a New Somerset And Dorset Railway company with the aim of eventually restoring the entire line. Similar projects are springing up around the country, as in the Helston Project, the Yorkshire Wolds Railway, the Bluebell Line, Peak Rail, the Aln Valley Railway and the Didcot, Newbury and Southampton line. The S & D line emerged in the 1850s and 1860s as a result of small local groups building stations, laying track, and eventually linking up. The prospect of something similar happening in the long-term future is slowly emerging.

I cycled back to Stourpaine along the Trailway. Unlike H.G. Wells' fictional hero, Mr. Hoopdriver, who sees a young woman cycling in her bloomers escaping from the clutches of unscrupulous older man and cycles after her in hot pursuit, I saw young Mums with pushchairs and a succession of speculating rooks and magpies.

For the past decade Sir Richard Branson, aware of the increased traffic on railways, has consistently advocated greater spending on railways, and yet Government continues to concentrate resources on roads and motor transport. This over-reliance on one approach is rigid and mechanistic. Cycle ways, railways and roads can co-exist, as in the Netherlands, Switzerland and parts of the US, and offer greater choice and relative safety. The type of thinking that blocks off different ways of being may be vested in capital. However, that analysis is relatively crude as it does not explain why there is this

21

cutting off or forgetting of more conducive options. It is as if some people are wired to a dualistic and monochrome world and yet others see alternative ways that take humanity to a better place.

I stopped to chat to Frank Bristow, who was walking to the Easter Egg Hunt, about the Station and Trailway, now filling up with more families on bicycles and voluptuous women joggers, and my forthcoming cycle ride from Clapham Common to Dorset in the manner of Edward Thomas' 1913 journey to explore that split and Englishness. His eyes lit up when I mentioned Englishness. 'That's important,' he said. 'It's something that I worry about and the Government seems to be ignoring the liberties that our ancestors struggled for.' With Frank's thoughts ringing in my ears, I cycled up Gains Cross and down into Stourpaine.

Chapter Two

Edward Thomas

One hundred years after it was written, *In Pursuit of Spring* (1914), with its combination of cycling, literary pilgrimage, strangeness and references to spring and the natural world, continues to beguile and inspire. When I reread this montage of stories, quotations, voices, literary criticism, digressions and odd juxtapositions, I knew that I had to emulate the journey and see what was left and who had subsequently lived along the route. I set about honing my appreciation of the man, his life and times in order to discover why he took the journey and wrote the book in the way that he did. I also wanted to understand the disarming way in which the book moves from the cheering to the dark and untangle the mysterious and disconcerting 'other man' and other oddities. The 'other man' is perhaps meant to be Thomas' alter ego and part of his struggle against depression. He surfaces throughout the narrative and clearly disturbs the narrator as well as the narrative. In fact, we know that Thomas cycled with his brother, Julian, and friend, Jessie Berridge, for parts of the journey. The travel book is thus a work of semi-fiction and it is the peculiarity of this unconventional book that requires contextualization.

Edward Thomas (1878-1917) was born in London to Welsh parents. His father was a Nonconformist, worked at the Board of Trade and was an active Liberal Party member. Thomas's first book, *The Woodland Life* (1897), was published before he won a history scholarship to Lincoln College,

Oxford. His Welsh and southwest English ancestral horizons attracted him to the natural world. He disliked London, apart from the commons, and lived precariously in rural southern England as a country writer, biographer, essayist and critic. He gradually established himself as a writer of reviews, writing and reading prodigiously in order to support his growing family. He produced more than thirty books, compiled sixteen editions and anthologies and wrote more than a million and a half words of review. By 1911 he had a breakdown from the psychological strain and the struggle to find greater creative freedom. Exhaustion overtook him as he wrote seven books that year. He underwent an early form of psychoanalysis and began writing about his life. He recovered in fits and starts to enhance his reputation as an astute poetry critic and country writer. His biographies of *Algernon Charles Swinburne* (1912) and *Walter Pater* (1914) outlined his ideas on using the rhythms of direct speech in poetry and prose. Retrospectively, we can see that he was an outstanding critic being the first to recognize the poetry of D.H. Lawrence, Ezra Pound and Robert Frost as well as praising the writing of Ford Madox Ford, W.H. Hudson, W.H. Davies and Walter de la Mare. The bulk of his writing however was as a close observer of country life, where he celebrated the historical and literary landscape, the natural world of each region and locality that he encountered as a source of Englishness, of re-discovery and celebration. Whilst this may be nostalgic, it is also a Wordsworthian methodology that is still an active part of our culture, as seen on television programmes that are concerned with walking and cycling the landscape. In this way, Thomas was not only continuing a tradition he was attempting to enhance it. Thomas was a driven man.

The journey, though, appears to be a search for understanding and the reason for that is seemingly not hard to find. The escalation of the 'organised insanity' of an arms race between the European powers dominated the news headlines of 1913 and early 1914. Russia stated her intention of quadrupling her army in anticipation of a show down with Germany. The First Lord of the Admiralty, Winston Churchill worked towards and managed to increase the navy budget. Admiral Alfred von Tirpitz in Germany boasted about the new warships that he was commissioning. There was a genuine fear that the Germans might invade and this was focusing much attention, worry and introspection. This undoubtedly impacted upon Thomas. Yet he is concerned with deeper matters and does not mention the fortified mobilization points at Box Hill and Henley Grove that he rides past.

In politics, the Government was pointedly worried about and trying to quell strikers, unionists, suffragettes, Irish republicans and the unemployed. The Suffragette movement, led by Emmeline Pankhurst, was becoming more proactive and engaged in a newsworthy and violent campaign to get their message across. At the June 1913 Derby, Emily Wilding Davison threw herself under the King's horse, Anmer, as it rounded Tattenham Corner and was killed. The movement, now in its third decade of activism, was an integral part in the undermining and transforming Victorian and Edwardian mores. Restraint in all aspects of life was becoming a thing of the past. This was doubtless impacting upon Thomas at conscious and unconscious levels.

In the arts, where Thomas mingled, the leading figures were clashing and the impending War does not seem to concern them. The artist and writer, Percy Wyndham Lewis, was attacking the smugness of British culture in his Vorticist journal, *Blast*, and his friend' Roger Fry, was raising public awareness of Post-Impressionism at Grafton Galleries and having a huge impact on design with the Omega Workshops at Fitzroy Studios. They had fallen out over a commission to provide wall decorations for the Daily Mail Ideal Home Exhibition. There was Russian triumph in opera and ballet at Drury Lane. Richard Wagner was making his first impact at Covent Garden. Igor Stravinsky's 'Rite of Spring', chiming with intense interest in paganism, Frederick Delius' 'On Hearing The First Cuckoo in Spring,' and Vaughan Williams' 'London Symphony' were premiered. Mrs. Patrick Campbell triumphed as a Cockney flower girl in George Bernard Shaw's new play, *Pygmalion*.

In the smaller world of poetry, where more or less everyone knew everyone else, the most popular work was John Masefield's *The Everlasting Mercy* (1911), whose coarseness resonated with popular taste. This bohemian world, centred upon Harold Monro's Poetry Bookshop, W.B. Yeats' gatherings at Woburn Buildings and T. E. Hulme's Soho soirees that Thomas dipped in and out of, had an atmosphere of moving forward through shock, uncertainty and imbibing difference. The London scene was a heady melting pot of the new and different.

Thomas commuted by train between southern England and the London digs where he wrote many of his books, essays and countless reviews. When in London he spent time at the Poetry Bookshop, the Square Club, and dined every Tuesday at the Mont Blanc restaurant in Soho, socialising with Edward Garnett, Joseph Conrad, W.H. Davies, Walter de la Mare, W.H. Hudson, D.H. Lawrence and others. He also frequented the Eustace Miles vegetarian restaurant in Chandos Street, with Bunny Garnett and Clifford Bax, where suffragettes mingled with avant-garde bohemians. Margaret Schlegel refers to it dismissively in E. M. Forster's *Howard's End*, where 'people come up to you and beg your pardon, but you have a beautiful aura.' We are beginning to see Thomas in a clearer light. He is close to the bohemian world of the suffragettes, difference, vegetarianism and paganism. I had to delve deeper.

This commuting life marked his mental map of places and allowed him to broaden his thinking of Englishness into an understanding of the importance of locality. This harks back to an Elizabethan concept with its history in the mapping and writing of England and allowed each localized attachment to have value. It is crucially not solely a literary version of Englishness but also a lived one. Thomas' passion for the natural world comes from localized works by Richard Jefferies, and Gilbert White's *The Natural History of Selborne*, from which he saw the need for fresh observation and the need to look with eyes wide open. This approach is intrinsically private and individual and far from the public domain of nationalists, politicians and ideologists and their views of England and Englishness.

As a boy Thomas had seen London swallow up the open

fields around Clapham. Urban sprawl was encroaching upon unkempt and untenanted farms. His hand-to-mouth existence as a freelance writer meant that he and his wife, Helen, always lived in rented accommodation. When they had children he couldn't write at home and so would rent a room elsewhere as an office. He was a nomad, working away from home researching and exploring, a wayfaring writer on the open road with the gypsies, vagrants, travellers and the other uneducated country people that William Wordsworth and Samuel Taylor Coleridge wrote about in their *Lyrical Ballads*.

The process of contextualization is like being a detective and asking questions. Other questions that I asked bore fruit. I discovered that Thomas was not alone in writing about literary pilgrimages and that Thomas had connections with the Suffragette movement. The now forgotten *In The Old Paths* (1913) by Scottish writer, Arthur Grant, in essence offers another version of English cultural identity forged from walking the footpaths of poets and writers in central England and the Midlands. Grant shared Thomas' love of history, churches, and graveyards, Jefferies, George Borrow and extolled pastoral England. His writing, for all its appeals to history and the literary, lacks the concentrated intensity and perversity of Thomas. It has more affection, particularly for Shakespeare, William Penn and the Quakers, Charles Lamb, Thomas Gray, William Shenstone, than disaffection finding 'tongues in trees, books in the running brooks, sermons in stones and good in everything.' It is looking backwards and less focused on the immediate whereas Thomas is manically looking ahead.

Independent women were fuelling this zest for the new as well as writing some of the most provocative material. Rebecca West's contribution to *Blast* concerns a man unhappily married to a woman who has a deeply sensuous nature and undisguised physical appetites. He follows her onto the moor one night in an attempt to confirm that she has a lover. When he discovers that her intention is an innocent midnight swim, he holds her head under the water until he believes her dead. They also occasioned fights between the most articulate of men. The classic example being Wyndham Lewis and Hulme's altercation over Kate Lechmere, Lewis' lover and partner in the Rebel Arts Centre. Lewis marched over to 67 Frith Street, where Hulme lived with Dolly Kibblewhite, to confront him. Lewis was dragged down the stairs and out into the garden in the centre of Soho Square. The fight ended when Hulme hung Lewis upside down on the iron railings surrounding the garden. Hulme and Lechmere subsequently had a passionate affair. Thomas at the time of his self-doubt and self-loathing was about to meet a young woman, Eleanor Farjeon, with whom he would fall in love.

Thomas was clearly a private man and within this world of intense networking he encountered such stormy characters as Ezra Pound, whose poetry he admired. The view, implied in Matthew Hollis' recent book, *Now All Roads Lead To France: The Last Years of Edward Thomas*, is that his journey is in part an escape from literary London at a time of anxiety and internal unrest only scratches at the surface. Pound, who described Thomas as 'a mild fellow with no vinegar in his veins,' was nothing to do with it. Thomas was clearly disturbed by many things. He perhaps wanted to break free of criticism and to be somehow more creative. He may have wanted to look at his own resources and bearings, to find that something new and chose a literary pilgrimage in several cycle rides and train journeys back to the world of Coleridge, Wordsworth and Jefferies. This conventional reading is insufficient to fully explain the quest and psychological disturbance that is echoed in the stories and strangeness of *In Pursuit of Spring*.

I discovered a plausible partial catalyst from the time he spent at Clifford Bax's at his Elizabethan manor house in Broughton Clifford, Wiltshire in April 1912. It was here that he was also treated by his psychoanalyst, Godwin Baynes and met, amongst the guests, his lover, Olive Hockin, an artist, pagan, skiing champion and militant Suffragette and her best friend, Eleanor Farjeon. Critics have tended to concentrate on his relationship with Farjeon and missed this other connection. Hockin was arrested on suspicion of firebombing the Chancellor of the Exchequer, Lloyd George's home, damaged the orchid house at Kew and subsequently burnt down Roehampton Golf Club, for which she was imprisoned in late 1913. She surely would have made an impression on Thomas, albeit on an unconscious level. Moreover, Baynes helped to instill some self-confidence in Thomas through talking and walking within a heady circle of intellectual pagans. Many of the circle were exploring intellectually and sexually. Bax, the brother of the composer, Arnold, was an artist turned playwright, deeply imbued in theosophy and mysticism. He was close to the 'other man' as a sandal wearing, nut eating, and ethical utopian. Thomas, Bax,

Farjeon and Hockin all contributed material to *Orpheus*, the journal of the Art Movement of the Theosophical Society, printed by the Women's Printing Society, between 1911 and 1914. Farjeon lived for a time in a Berkshire wood with Hockin and recounts an incident when they went skinny dipping in a lake, finding Baynes had swum to middle of the lake before them, worshipping the deity and leaving a crown of wild parsley. Thomas subsequently visited the woods and lake. Hockin was deeply pagan and believed that she could see the spirits and figures that she painted. Her blue and green watercolour, *Pan, Dryads and Nymphs* (exhibited at the Royal Academy in 1914) has a watery feel suffusing a woodland scene of pan-worship. Given Thomas's involvement with the Bax set, it seems plausible that their spiritual, artistic and psychological thinking was absorbed by Thomas and helped form the quest and disturbances that make *In Pursuit of Spring*.

Moreover, when Thomas introduced Eleanor to his wife Helen, Helen accepts her in spiritual and mystical terms and sees the union as a means of retrieving Thomas. Helen recounts the three of them arm in arm breathlessly entering a copse in moonlight and tense expectation. Out of the silence they hear a nightingale. 'Low and tender it is at first, but as it draws out the sweetness becomes strength, the tenderness passion, until in that wild note it is as if God speaks and we understand, but what we understand we do not know. All pain, all ecstasy, all despair, all love expressed.' Edward kisses Helen and Helen tells him to kiss Eleanor, which he does, and their mutual understanding and union is blessed. This beautiful evocation strikes me as a scene not unlike Hockin's watercolour with Thomas as Pan and Helen and Eleanor as the wood nymphs. There is a beguiling synchronicity.

The other catalyst is that Thomas realised that local attachments were found on location, at their source, as well as in memorial inscriptions and literary writing. *In Pursuit of Spring* is a book about looking for signs in the fullest sense. The theme of fertility and finding the source of English life is recurrent in mentioning of fountains, rivers and springs. This fear of loss as well as a celebration of what remains underpins the work of the walking / cycling poet as much today as a century ago when Thomas cycled from Clapham Common to Salisbury, and later from Salisbury to the Quantocks, in a quest to see where Coleridge 'fed on honey-dew and drank the milk of Paradise.' It's the source of its importance and why it has continuing relevance to the idea of Englishness.

It is possible to see the journey as something of a spiritual journey with self-renewal as the ultimate aim. Thomas notes each bird, birdsong, river, stream, woodland and tree as survivors and celebrates their and his bond with nature in a writing tradition that goes back deep into English history via Jefferies, Jane Austen, Wordsworth, Gilbert White, Daniel Defoe to Michael Drayton, Edmund Spenser and beyond. There is a comic literary forebear to this journey that Thomas would have known well and that is H.G. Wells' *Wheels of Chance* (1895), which similarly describes the birdsong as the protagonist cycles south out of London. Wells' satirical novel shows how the bicycle was weakening the English class structure and fuelling female emancipation. Here a frustrated draper's assistant escapes into a fantasy world, rescues a young woman in distress and cycles through Surrey and Hampshire with her.

After a long harsh winter of personal and literary struggles, Thomas found his spring in a profusion of honeysuckle and began to find his new self as a poet. The honeydew, with its effects of 'wildness and richness, purity and softness' that nourished Coleridge nourished him and by implication it will nourish you and me.

Chapter Three

The Aftermath

Edward Thomas did not start seriously writing poetry until December 1914 after his friend the American poet, Robert Frost, suggested that some parts of *In Pursuit of Spring* might be turned into poems using the same cadence and style. He wrote one hundred and forty poems in the last two years of his life, which now forms the basis of his reputation as one of the great English poets of the twentieth century. Thomas' creative release begins with the cycle ride and although his reputation lies with the poems this rather obscures the true nature of his work as an explorer and observer of the English and Welsh countryside.

Thomas was an inheritor and purveyor of the English tradition of nature writing and someone who, in a life cut short by a shell-blast at Arras on 9 April 1917, solidified in twenty years of cycling and walking a path through the conflicting versions of national identity. His writing helped prepare the way for a version of Englishness without the Empire, Parliament, a rigid class structure and racial superiority as its backbone. It looks to the countryside, the natural world and its inhabitants, as the true custodians of past, present and future England and Englishness, whilst acknowledging the place of London, in *The Heart of England*, with its pockets of wild places, as a cog in a wider and deeper wheel.

It is hard to assess the full impact of Thomas on our idea of Englishness. Its gradual cultural acceptance is to be found in the losses of two World Wars and Empire as well as the tensions between being rooted and rootless. In the summer of 1995 I was driven into the Hampshire countryside to meet a judge, by the late, Muir Hunter QC, a leading bankruptcy barrister and a co-founder of Amnesty International. This Hampshire judge believed in the interpreting common law for the individual. He had made some far-reaching decisions on divorce and pension law and ensured that the general public understood how he had reached his judgments. Scrupulously fair, he was often a thorn in the side of the Establishment and had the capacity for vision, foresight and dissent. He was probably the best known judge of the twentieth century and had I known where we going I would have been nervous before meeting him. He often acknowledged when the law was an ass and that he had to make judgments with which were against his will, such as Miller v. Jackson [1977] QB 966, when he was forced to stop Linz Cricket Club from playing cricket because a house owner objected to cricket balls arriving unannounced in her back garden.

As a young man, he had been in favour of capital punishment and revised his views seeing the practice as unethical and open to error. His judgments were exceptionally well written, even humorous, in simple sentences of clear language so that everyone could understand the thinking behind the decision. Alfred Denning was 95 years old when we met briefly in his modest home. I recall Muir confusing me with another poet friend who had gone to Magdalen College, Oxford and, lacking the space for correction, let it ride. We thus briefly spoke about his student days at Oxford before his attention was monopolized with legal conversation.

Muir, whose forensic skills and mastery of detail in corruption cases had led to the resignation of a Tory Home Secretary, could be an insensitive man. I recall advising him that one of our guests at a poetry event had recently lost her son, through suicide, and he continued to talk about death until the poor woman was driven to distraction and fled the room in tears. Denning was cut of finer, more sensitive cloth. He put me at my ease immediately with a broad smile and ordered tea. Frail and dependent upon two walking sticks, there was much movement in his eyes as we chatted. He placed his chin above his fingers on top of his walking stick with elbows on the table and listened attentively to Muir's long preamble and spoke only to clarify. He had a wonderful Hampshire accent and cheeky grin. He acknowledged that had it not been for the Great War taking away many of the most talented of his generation he may not have risen to become Master of the Rolls. He endearingly called himself one of the runts of the College litter. Our collective loss he argued was considerable. 'We lost,' he said, 'some of our most talented people and, don't forget, they died for England.' This statement of great modesty has always stayed with me. Denning was an endearing and modest man. Sharp and able, something of a Jonathan Swift to Muir's Squire Bramble.

A quick illustration of that loss can be gauged by considering the composer, George Butterworth, acknowledged by Ralph Vaughan Williams as the best of his generation. A sniper shot

Butterworth through the head at the Battle of the Somme in August 1916. Twice awarded the Military Cross for gallantry in trench warfare for the Durham Light Infantry, Butterworth had destroyed many compositions he deemed inadequate before leaving for France. His music was complex yet extremely simple and sparing, and imbued with an Englishness derived from folk song and the underscoring of melody.

Butterworth was greatly involved in the collection and annotation of folk songs and folk dances, especially Morris, which he helped revive, from 1909 onwards. He co-wrote *The Country Dance Book* (1912, 16) with Cecil Sharp. A cricketer and professional folk dancer, his orchestral works include 'Two English Idylls' (1911), ' A Shropshire Lad, a rhapsody' (1912) and 'The Banks of Green Willow, an idyll' (1913). He also wrote choral music and song settings of Shelley and Housman poems. He was close friends with Vaughan Williams, Gustav Holst and Adrian Boult and intimately involved with the revival of English music based upon folk song. His delicate compositions indicate a subtle sonic imagination that was full of promise before his death.

Thomas was keen on the folk song revival movement from near its outset and edited *The Pocket Book of Poems and Songs for the Open Air* (1907). This anthology of walking ballads links his interests in poetry, folk song and walking. Both are democratic and cultivate a sense of cultural identity and belonging. Folk singing and dancing at home, school and in pubs were considerably revived after the Great War.

37

I do not drive. I walk, cycle, travel by public transport and taxis. This way of life allows me to connect more with people and the natural world. I hear and listen to local stories. I am writing this at a time of the loss of biodiversity, especially amongst birds, insects, bees and of woodlands and wild spaces, and when our agriculture and the skills of working the land on which we depend for our food, clothing and other necessities, is in decline. There is a continual battle against Government to recognise and support the added value of conservation. Thomas shows that by walking and cycling the outdoors, exploring the natural world, connecting with its waterways, woodland and wild places we connect with self and the past in the present and by so doing move forward. It is healthy and not alienating. It helps us to re-connect with our locality and to our selves and others. This morning I have just returned from the Stourpaine shop in the pub and saw an otter by the river bridge, which I have warmly reported to friends and housemates, who will doubtless now have another reason to walk to the river way to the pub and shop.

Thomas helped popularize Jefferies as a prophet of nature who derived nourishment from his childhood haunts and thus linked location and walking the outdoors with wellbeing. He stressed attachment rather than detachment to your roots, location and its people. His poetry obliquely connects the Great War with broader questions of human existence, survival, memory and 'home.' It is characterized by the use of counterpoint. Positive and negative images mingle. His 'Home' poems negotiate a beguiling interplay of desire and denial, alienation and allegiance, yearning and dispossession. Rich in detail, his poetry carries a love of the English landscape that continues to resonate. Thomas, though, to use Raymond Williams' phrase in *The Country and the City* 'came to the country' and was not part of the struggle of rural life and is perhaps one step away from its inner turmoil. His contribution to the walking and open spaces movement anticipates the modern tensions between mobility and home. Consider the many opposites in his poems, as in the tree, relatively fixed in place, and the bird, capable of flight and migration. Similarly, the relative stability of the wood is in contrast to the relative mobility and meandering nature of the footpath. Dislocation and displacement are visible in his poems through the figure of the travelling man / narrator and the movement of gypsies. The poem 'Haymaking' shows the workers 'out of the reach of change.' Comparable to a Constable painting, it describes a momentary stasis within rural labour and through its use of detail impresses upon the reader the age of the scene and its need for preservation.

> The men leaned on their rakes, about to begin,
> But still. And all were silent. All was old,
> This morning time, with a great age untold.
> Older than Clare and Cowper, Morland and Crome,

The references are to a time older than the rural poets and painters cited and 'all' being inclusive of the wild life and buildings and implying that nothing should be lost. The poem ends with an appeal to immortality 'in a picture of an old grange' reinforcing the idea that 'all was old' with the detail that the farm was once a grange.

In 1798 William Hazlitt famously walked 150 miles to Nether Stowey to visit Coleridge and Wordsworth and described in his essay, 'My First Acquaintance With Poets' how Coleridge 'liked to compose in walking over uneven ground, or breaking through the straggling branches of a copse-wood; whereas Wordsworth always wrote (if he could) walking up and down a straight gravel walk, or in some spot where the continuity of his verse met with no collateral interruption.' John Keats walked 642 miles during his 1818 tour of the Lakes and Scotland in the belief that it would help his poetry more than staying at home among his books. Thomas inherited the walking ideology of the Romantics, more from Hazlitt than Wordsworth who differed in their assessment of the impact of walking. Crucially, though, he augmented his 'tramping' with cycling, with its greater immediacy and quicker recovery and movement of self. Hazlitt summarized this as follows: 'With change of place we change our ideas; nay our opinions and feelings ....We cannot enlarge our conceptions; we only shift our point of view.' This happens he explains because 'the mind can form no larger idea of space than the eye can take in at a single glance ... Things near us are seen of the size of life: things at a distance are diminished to the size of understanding.' The life renewing benefits that Hazlitt assigns to limited perception through walking are clearly hastened by cycling. In this way Thomas knowingly moves towards a more urgent sense of recovered self and communality that chimes with post-modern experience.

In Pursuit of Spring carries more substance and depth as a journey into the heart of England on subsequent readings. It is surely a spiritual journey with the capacity for altered perceptions and one that clearly began an important transformation for him leading to his own flowering as a poet as well as contributing to our own understanding, coming out of deep social change following the Great War and the Suffragette movement, of what it is to be English. It pulls together, albeit in disturbed writing, a living conception and love of Englishness that has survived and been added to since his life was ended so abruptly.

Chapter Four

Bushes Farm

On the morning of 10 April, I cycled uphill to the remote Bushes Farm, on the Bushes Road, north of Stourpaine, where Lucy and Doreen Ridout have made a ramshackle, working farm into a thriving community. There is stables to the left, a small builder's yard to the right, another stables on the left and farm buildings on the right that have rented out as workshops to various businesses. Free range hens and ducks wander about. Beyond the workshops and the Ridouts' home on the left is an extensive caravan and camping site. Randomly parked motor vehicles line both sides of the main thoroughfare. This novel and effective land use for riding and engineering is a tenacious response to the loss of traditional agricultural pursuits by two intrepid ladies. When I look at Lucy's broad smile, ruddy cheeks and stout nose, I see one of the extended Ridout family that has deep historical roots in Okeford Fitzpaine, Fiddleford and Sturminster Newton. My character, Willy, from *The Willy Poems*, was part of this large extended family. In the eighteenth century, the Ridouts were horse rustlers, smugglers and tenant farmers and have shown an enterprising spirit as well as feisty temper over the years. In common with the Clarke, Corben, Lambert, Pope, Ricketts, Rose, Strange, Trowbridge, White, Woolridge and Yeatman families they have contributed the core population of Okeford Fitzpaine for the past five hundred years.

I arrived, under heavy cloud and threat of rain, having messaged my friend, Louise, congratulating her on taking affirmative action against her University for not paying her for three months. She and others are going to unleash their inner Divas outside the authorities offices and if that doesn't work she has threatened a one-woman show of *Joseph and his Amazing Technicolor Dream Coat*, or wailing. Leon's workshop is to the right of Lucy's bungalow, a weeping willow and ornamental pond garden lined by two old ploughs and a seed drill that beguile as sculptures sunk into the soil. Cocks crow continuously and there is a sense of the past living in the present throughout. A braying donkey is heard within a melodious sequence of birdsong provided by blackbirds, starlings, hedge sparrows, wrens, tits and finches. Goats look out longingly from an old calf shed.

The workshop is a mechanical engineer's Aladdin's cave of vintage and classic car motoring and garage equipment. This extraordinary working museum piece has been accumulated by one of my oldest friends, Leon, whom I have known since I was six. His showroom is decorated with enamel advertising signs for Wills Gold Flake Cigarettes, Continental Motor Cycle Tyres, Duckham's Motor Oil, Exide Batteries, Michelin, Shell, Guinness, Goodyear, Morris and an Accidents of All Kinds & Illnesses by the Railways Passengers Assurance Co hoarding. A superbly detailed late Fifties Italian Gilera motorcycle dominates. The Gilera 125, straddled by a blindfolded buxom brunette and her smiling lover, gleams. Two original Esso petrol pumps stand by the frame of a vintage car, which is surrounded by an assortment of lathes, presses, forge and work benches covered with hammers, clamps, vices, rivets, hose clips, hacksaws and fan belts. Beyond this is the main workshop where seven vintage cars, motorcycles and lawnmowers are in various states of disrepair. The sound of blackbirds nesting in the roof and the drip of water from a tiny hole in the roof produces a memorable ambience. It is like a neo-Dickensian version of *The Darling Buds of May* with soundtrack by Tom Waits out of *American Graffiti* and Leon appearing as a latter-day bovver boy or, as he puts it, the old git.

I should say at this point that Leon is an avid theatre lover and has a solid memory of West End plays and actors. Leon's card says that he is a Classic Car and Vintage Vehicle Automotive Engineer. The description does not cover his mind and mien. He can break down and reassemble engines and has a visual mind. As a mechanic, he is used to breaking things down in order to discover how they work. He applies this method to other areas of life and has a radical perspective on most things. Seeing quite deeply, he swings from the monosyllabic succinct to the lilting rant or rhapsodic in engaging twists and turns. He is a good poker player, adept at disarming thugs and timewasters. We sat next to each other at school for nine years and for part of that time had an excellent English teacher, Mr. Clark, who gave us both a love of language and literature. Leon says that 'Bonzo' Clark had predicted that we would have vocabularies of 20,000 - 25,000 words, one-third less than his own vocabulary.
'No way,' I said.
'You certainly make up for my deficiencies,' he replied, picking up a wrench with serious intent. He always likes to have something in his hands.
'I talk loads and have lots of useless clever words. All the Latinates. I prefer the simplicity of Anglo-Saxon brevity

though. You know, the common touch.' My father always used to have a pencil on his right ear. I invariably have a pen on mine.

'You are common,' he smirked.

'Thank you,' I smiled. 'I can be non-verbal, use gesture and my eyes a lot. I try to use words carefully and fail as often as not. Bonzo was on the money in terms of the amount of words people use now.'

'Yes.' said Leon as he moved the wrench along his hand and led the way to his desk. We finalized our travel arrangements over OS maps and mugs of tea as the heavens opened. An orchestra of percussionists playing on the roof.

I cycled home to Portman Lodge, noting the first signs of gorse and recalling that Bushes Farm had been the site of the Great Dorset Steam Fair for a quarter of a century. Begun in 1968 by a group of local steam enthusiasts after showing a cine film of the last days of the S & D Railway at the skittle alley of the Royal Oak pub, Okeford Fitzpaine. It was then known as the Stourpaine Bushes Steam Fair. With John Garrett, Ted Hines, Johnny Antell, Walt Trowbridge, Arthur 'Happy' Field, Giles Romanes, Betty Marsh and Sammy Russell, agricultural and engineering figures from my childhood, Mike Oliver considerably expanded the event from a local steam and country fair into a five day event on a 600 acre site attracting 200,000 people. A population of 25,000 people lives on site for the best part of a week. The traditional nighttime line up of more than 200 showman engines and heavy haulage circuit around the site is an awesome spectacle supported by six entertainment pavilions and countless beer and cider tents. The only local comparable event as a national institution is the Glastonbury Festival, at Pilton in Somerset. The Steam Fair, bringing in much needed local income, is now also known as the National Heritage Show in recognition of it being one of Europe's largest outdoor events.

In the morning I loaded my bicycle into the back of Leon's Rover and we drove off towards London bright and early. His vintage Rover has such a smooth engine with the sensation of travelling at 30 mph when you are in fact travelling at twice the speed. At least, that's what I expected. Instead Leon drove to Bushes Farm where we were to be joined by Rob, a mutual friend and filmmaker. My face and jaw dropped. Rob and I had worked together years ago recording some comedy drama scripts that I had written until he fell in love with an Anglo-Spanish beauty, Melissa, and he was nowhere to be found. Rob has a heart of gold, is very well meaning and thoroughly unreliable. We had spoken by phone of the possibility of filming my cycle ride. It seemed highly unlikely now, as the day before he was in Newport collecting a passport and bound for Ireland, that he would be joining us. 'Is he really coming?' I asked. 'Yes,' Leon emphatically replied, 'he's coming.' I had not prepared a script. Eeeek! Indeed I had laughed out loud when Leon announced that Rob might be coming along to film our outing. Rob is always trying and failing to do the impossible. He has little concept of time and works whatever hours suit him regardless of need and circumstances. I put the chances of seeing Rob at any time that month at a million to one. A few months back we had spent half a day following his trail and never caught up with him. After half an hour of waiting,

I was getting itchy, looking at my watch, checking to see if I had a message on my phone. At last and to my astonishment Rob's car appeared. With a wide-eyed smile, Rob loaded his bags of equipment into the back, slid himself into the only available space left, gave us both some sweets and we were off towards Ringwood and Clapham.

Our first unscheduled stop was for Leon's full English breakfast at an out of the way truckers' gaffe. An hour later we were on the motorway to Portsmouth about forty miles in the wrong direction from the A31 where I thought we were going. I plucked up courage to doubt the directions of former long distance lorry driver Leon and consulted the road atlas. I began mentally writing a script in my head.

Rob had used his time in Newport the day before to follow a story about the town council attempting to claim council tax from boat owners moored in the harbour. He had filmed an angry boat owner who was spearheading the legal defence of what appeared to be an extreme measure to obtain more tax from a tenuous link to town facilities. I recalled my visit to a wonderful junior school at Blaina, near Abergavenny, in Gwent during the boom years and shock at the boarded shops in the high street and failure to find more than one place to eat at lunchtime. I noted that by comparison we lived in the prosperous South of the country. Leon shot me a look and said that I should never underestimate the extent of poverty and lack of facilities in the rural South. Our chat continued through Leon's experiences of corruption and justice in Italy. The Italians, it seems, tolerate a degree of openness towards corruption that is unusual by local standards where everyone knows that an unethical company has bribed local officials for building planning permission. There is considerable anger and no redress without adequate and unavailable proof. It is one of the dark arts. Leon recalled a wayward son of the Mafia that had sowed his wild oats too liberally for the Catholic Church and got caught stealing the wife and other items from an upstanding, devout politician. The man was given a hefty sentence to satisfy the Catholics and allowed to serve it in his own home to satisfy the Mafia. His visitors were selectively monitored; otherwise he could continue his nefarious activities.

We failed to find Nightingale Lane, Clapham, the start of Thomas' journey. It was not just my poor eyesight and map reading. I blame inadequate signage. I found Clapham Common and thus considered it close enough. I cycled what I believed was the old London road, although to be honest I was only sure that I was heading in the right direction, and found the experience somewhat alarming. I was concentrating on cycling suitably quickly and watching out for parked vehicles, red buses, lorries and traffic lights. Thomas only had to contend with dozens of other cyclists filling the road. I stopped several times to ask directions and of those who bothered to stop to help no one knew the name of the road as opposed to the street name. I cycled on. Finally I saw a sign that I was on Kingston Road confirming that I was on the A24. My heart felt better. I had wanted to stop at Nonsuch Park, the last surviving part of Henry VIII's deer hunting park surrounding the former Nonsuch Palace. The park contains Nonsuch Park House, built in the mid-eighteenth century, which Thomas would have seen, but as time was pressing I cycled on. Thomas cycled around the park finding a fountain and cross commemorating Charlotte Farmer, who died in 1906 and ignored the remnants of the palace gardens.

Given the realization that most of the early part of Thomas' journey out of London had been annihilated by nondescript urbanization, it was agreed that we should meet at Epsom registry office and proceed down the A24 to Dorking and Box Hill. It was at the Epsom registry office that George Harrison had married Pattie Boyd in 1966. George's classic songs, 'Something' and 'I Need You,' written for Pattie, and 'Here Comes The Sun' were composed in and around the Surrey hills. Pattie Boyd also inspired Eric Clapton's 'Layla,' 'Wonderful Tonight' and other love songs. It hadn't much to do with Edward Thomas, who cycled by, or the theme of my book. However, it gave me a chance to cycle and gave Rob something to film. I needed some water and to stretch my legs.

After the tenth cycle around the parking place in front of the grade 11 listed building, once the home of Lady Jane Ashley, of whom most of central Epsom is named after, I was beginning to hit the stop on which I was supposed to stop and get off my bicycle. I finally managed this and said my lines. Rob was pleased and liked everything apart from the fact that I lifted up my trousers upon getting off my bicycle. Off I cycled again. This time I was moving my head too much and the next time my eyes were looking away from the camera. A crowd had gathered to watch my pratfalls. Leon was guffawing. I was beginning to wish that I could cycle off down the road to Ashtead and the Leg of Mutton and Cauliflower, which Thomas mentioned. In 1913 he cycled past Epsom common, much smaller now, through the town and onwards with a hedge less gorse-land either side of the road and then an oak copse down the road to Ashtead. There is now no gorse or copse. It is fully urban and the road heavily congested all the way to The Street. Thomas called it 'inhospitable' and that description still applies. Rob wanted some shots of my cycling down the road to the pub. I obliged several times, having been too fast three times and moving and suffering from a wobbling head before finally I joined Leon sitting outside the pub. The pub has also functioned as a farmhouse, a coroner's court, jailhouse and post office and has a plaque with a list of landlords dating back to 1741. The Leg did not impress Rob and Leon and has known better days. No longer the hub of the community, it is an old time boozer with wooden floorboards and seems to be lacking in sawdust for a more authentic feel. It is empty of soul. Two old men at the bar were having a vintage argument about Mrs. Thatcher and old Labour. We could have been in 1981. The prospect of a fight between the old guys going at hammer and tongs was tangible until one let slip the beginning of a smirk. Rob suggested that they were on the payroll as local entertainers. Leon finished his drink and noted that the country hasn't progressed at all since the days of the milk snatcher.

Before a fight broke out we headed for Leatherhead Bridge and the fifteenth century Running Horse pub at Bridge Street. We crossed a bridge on the A24 and found no pub. I checked Google, the pub was still standing, just not adjacent to the current bridge or it was well camouflaged. The Running Horse, originally known as Rummings House, has a plaque commemorating John Skelton's poem about Elinore Rumming that Thomas cited. We couldn't make the Sat Nav work, our exact location was at the bottom of OS Map 146 and not apparent on OS map 145 and after a fruitless search decided to aim for Burford Bridge at Box Hill. I don't think that Daniel Defoe had this sort of trouble when he travelled this way in 1723.

The river Mole crosses the North Downs between Dorking and Leatherhead, where it cuts a steep-sided valley through chalk called the Mole Valley. My first sight of the Mole was as a fast flowing river. It is mentioned in Drayton's *Poly-Olbion* (1612), Milton's description of 'the sullen Mole' was echoed by Pope in *Windsor Forest* (1713) and Bloomfield's *Wild Flowers* (1806) notes the Mole Valley, with its wild banks, 'where the Mole all silent glides / Dwells Peace – and Peace is wealth to me.' Since its heavily polluted days in the second half of the last century it has been cleaned. The Mole dried up in the summer of 1976 between Leatherhead and Dorking. Now it has a rich diversity of fish and on this day has ferocity. In 1913 Thomas had a choice of roads, which is denied the modern traveller of the A24. The road that he took would have been an old track to the left and south of the current A 24 through wooded hills, Leatherhead Downs, Mickleham Downs to Juniper Hill and Box Hill and on to Burford Bridge. We are now in the Surrey Hills, an area of Special Scientific Interest, and great beauty. I had a burning desire to get off the A24 and cycle inland far away from the incessant traffic roar.

Thomas cycled on pre-tarmacked road and his fellow travellers were mostly other cyclists. He entered Mickleham alone except for a horseman and his dog. This is the first country figure that Thomas saw that day and his description indicates that the man denotes a relic from rural Mickleham. He was 'a thick, stiff man in gray-coloured rough clothes' begaitered and carrying an ash-plant instead of a riding whip on a piebald pony. Smoking a pipe of strong, good tobacco, Thomas believes that he could help him understand the concept of resurrection of the just and divisions within society before death. He writes down an epitaph confusing 'Time was these ashes lov'd' with the 'lived' of the original, indicative of a man connecting spring with love more than living. It is a line that he quotes in stark isolation without commentary and the reader is left to ponder this psychic overflow. Within the range of possible meaning he perhaps is acknowledging his own search is for a deeper love. I don't know. It is one of several quirks that make the book fruitfully beguiling. When I first went to the Dorset Steam Fair it was dotted by bewhiskered figures dressed in old-fashioned country clothes still pursuing lives that were deeply imbedded in old rural customs that connected back to a distant past. These were residual people that had more in common with the pre-television age and resisting that which they did not need. Many of my early poems stemmed from conversations with such people. One illiterate man began his working life as a bird-scarer, became a stone hauler as roads were modernized, returned from the Second World War to become a road labourer and ended up working for the milk marketing board as a cheese maker, which was where I met him as an eighteen year old. Their contemporary equivalents are in the pre-computer age and refusing the so-called technological advances for a peace of mind. Thomas did not speak to the man on horseback, although he had questions that he wanted to ask. He is alienated from him by education and social division. He declines a possible living story, an offshoot, for the theme of resurrection and follows him into Mickleham. It is the kind of choice that Robert Frost indicates in his famous poem, 'The Road Not Taken,' and the kind of psychic material from reading Thomas that informed the making of the poem.

I cycled at speed along the dual carriageway down to Burford Bridge, concentrating on the fast traffic, for some time before I saw the remains of a former lane, slowed down causing a series of horn blasts, stopped and crossed the grass verge to the safer unmarked and possibly undesignated cycleway. Rob took some shots along this route and in a dugout layby north of the Burford Bridge Hotel that served as the entrance to a series of paths up the wooded hill. As Leon slept and Rob setup, I engaged in conversation with various walkers, including a rough looking, unshaven young man carrying cans of beer who was already under the influence of more than alcohol. There were others that seemed 'tired and emotional' and then a long-legged twenty-something in hot pants, veined tights and generous cleavage approached by an adjacent path walking her pooch and suddenly the place began to empty. I worried about her safety, as she was dressed so enticingly and about to walk into dense woodland. I concluded that she must have felt safe and hoped that her dog was less docile than he appeared. Perhaps she was on a rendezvous or merely one of the dozens of unemployed taking the air that day between the showers without a care in the world?

Chapter Five

Box Hill

I couldn't resist walking Box Hill, named after the ancient box woodland on the west of chalk slopes overlooking the Mole and so Leon and I set off up the steep and muddy footpath from Burford Bridge. The alternative route is from Westhumble, where the novelist, Fanny Burney, once lived. Burney, who was an inspiration to Jane Austen, married a French émigré, General D'Arblay, at St. Michael's Church, Mickleham in 1793. Burney has become better known in recent years thanks to the desire to study more women writers in the Romantic period. Best known as Samuel Johnson's friend and as a Diarist, the early studies of her life situated her within the English pastoral, extolled her Court connections (she was Second Keeper of the Robes for Queen Caroline) and presented her as a gifted letter writer, authoress and homemaker. We soon discovered that even on a wet, grey afternoon the Hill attracts a good many walkers and is a hot spot for cyclists. Later in the summer the road climb featured prominently in the Olympic Cycling races and subsequently cyclists came en masse to test themselves against the Olympic climb. Thomas cycled by seemingly without much of a glance upwards.

Box Hill became a popular destination for Londoners to visit from the mid-seventeenth century onwards and is mentioned by John Evelyn, Samuel Pepys and others as the place to visit for pleasure after taking the waters at Epsom. According to Defoe, by the 1720s, Box Hill had become a rendezvous to

take the air and 'divert, or debauch, or perhaps both.'
Discreet meetings could be arranged in and around Box Hill
on the pretext of taking the air. Admiral Lord Nelson met his
mistress, and painter, George Romney's muse, Lady Emma
Hamilton at the Burford Bridge Hotel before he vanquished
that Franco-Spanish fleet and met his death at the Battle of
Trafalgar in 1805. John Keats escaped from London to work
on his poem 'Endymion' at the Hotel in November 1818.
The contrast between the then fame of Nelson and Emma
Hamilton and that of Keats and his love, Fanny Brawne
could not be greater. Now the love letters exchanged between
Keats and Fanny are amongst the most famous ever written.
Box Hill has been and still is inextricably linked in the
popular imagination with love and relationships.

I was soon imbibing the scent of wild privet, keeping my eyes
out for the common-spotted orchids, which eventually
appeared, bluebells and moschatel, which sadly did not, and
looking forward to the prospect of the panoramic view to
come. I associate bluebells and moschatel with first love. I
picked bluebells, redolent of sultriness, for my first love,
Chris, and recall how I was excited into a breathless passion
by her perfume that she divertingly said was soap and years
later I identified as an earthy musk derived from moschatel. I
still don't know if she was keeping her perfumery a secret or
possessed a rather unusual and pre-Lush soap. Memory,
attached to place and feeling, and scent go hand in hand as
much as any other sense. Like a couple of stags, we were
leaving scents, footprints and other signs of our presence
along the path and adding our stories to those that had
preceded us and for those that would follow.

My mind drifted to one of the great love songs of the past thirty years, Richard Thompson's '1952 Vincent Black Lightning' and its star crossed lovers Red Molly and James. I began singing until Leon advised that I was upsetting the birds. 'Stop treading on the orchids,' he said. To get off the subject of my myopia, I told him the story of Fairport Convention, Sandy Denny and the Albion Band, and Thompson's relationship, with his first wife, Linda. Leon recalled liking the brass band section of Richard and Linda's stirring hit song, 'I Want To See The Bright Lights.' Leon pointed out at the Burford Bridge Hotel had been a bikers mecca in the Eighties, which I didn't know and that a 1952 Vincent Black Lightning had been the fastest motorcycle in the world, capable of a top speed of 150 mph / 240 kmh. It is now worth more than £100,000. In the recessionary Eighties, James had to become a robber to afford the motorbike and didn't mind dying for the love of Red Molly. The apogee of his life was riding to Box Hill on a 52 Vincent with a red headed girl seated behind him. Red hair and black leather were James' favourite colour scheme. Shot in the chest for armed robbery, he was 'running out of road,' 'running out of breath.' On his deathbed, he tells Red Molly: 'Now Norton's and Indians and Greaves' won't do, / Ah, they don't have a soul like a Vincent 52.' Finally, he gives her one last kiss and dies and gives her his Vincent to ride. Thompson sets the song in a traditional English melody and structure but plays the song stridently in an American folk song style. He thus evokes the romance of the motorbike within the cultural context of Chatterton, Bo Diddley, Barry MacSweeney, Jim Morrison and other poets and songwriters that died young.

As I was about to untangle the literary connections that had led people to Box Hill, Leon began recalling his frozen journeys to Yeovil College by motorbike in midwinter. He couldn't wait to own his first car and soon retired from motor biking. We fell silent. I looked for moschatel and only saw the ubiquitous gorse. I once made gorse wine to see if the coconut bouquet of the flower would come through into the wine. It tasted better than I anticipated even without the hint of coconut that I had hoped for. Soon there was enough early gorse for gallons of wine and the view came upon me like a scarlet woman.

It is the impact of Jane Austen's greatest work, *Emma*, with its interplay of understatement, revelation and latent sexual tension, and its most famous scene, the disastrous picnic that has led readers to Box Hill. Austen knew the area well, living down the road at Chawton from 1809 until her death and went on an exploring party there in 1814. She chose to use the name of the hill rather than give it an imaginary one and draw attention to the name and association of the place. 'Box' encompasses the verbal sparring of her characters, led by Emma Woodhouse, who has 'never been in love; and does not think it is her way or nature.' There is also a sense of claustrophobia, as in being 'boxed in,' implicated as well. *Emma* is a story of untamed match making and its achievement is to present an unresolved reading of desire. It is the need for understanding and resolution that has led people to visit Box Hill. The novel revolves around an extraordinary number of evasions, deceptions and mistakes that are presented by a seemingly precise, judgmental and authoritative narrator. The pivotal moment of the novel is played out at the Box Hill picnic, in summer heat and understated emotional and dramatic charge. There is a strange separateness and range of possible meanings played out at Box Hill that trips the reader. Frank blatantly flirts with Emma, enjoying the deception while Jane looks on, secretly wounded, secretly engaged, and Knightley, surreptitiously in love with Emma, watches jealously. Emma calls upon the box, being the place where the ladies are seated at the theatre, to perform to her tune and is shown to be 'unfeeling' towards Miss Bates and subsequently confronted by Knightley and taken to task. Emma consequently begins to change and grow, realizing how much she craves Knightley.

Emma is full of deception, where things mean something other or more for both characters and the reader. It is at once a dramatic depiction and puzzle of the English mind. What is seemingly precise and reserved has something other beneath its exterior. Sexual tension surfaces and is not quite contained. The limitation of self-discipline is exposed. A modern version of this would doubtless be a comedy of embarrassment with all its attendant disturbance and lack of resistance bubbling over.

Watching the 1996 movie of *Emma* adds to this pivotal scene. The experience of eating in a beautiful setting where orchids, butterflies and flowers proliferate and the views are spectacular appeals to both the eye and palate. The film shows the considerable organization involved in arranging teams of horses to transport wagons with picnickers, servants, food and outdoor furniture. The servants are constantly working to provide a leisurely outing and

59

moveable feast. This has the reward of the creating new relationships between the participants, the picturesque setting and cultural ideals. What is being consumed here is not just food. It is perhaps more fully viewed as an ethical act that serves to create cultural relations and identities. Certainly Emma is recreated as a result of the picnic.

I had not thought much about the origins of the picnic, which stems from the French 'pique nique' and aristocrats dining outside during a hunt, until seeing the film and rereading the novel's conflicting attitudes to picnicking. The narrator and Emma reject the picnic as an improper, vulgar modern taste. According to the OED, a new definition of the picnic emerged in the first two decades of the nineteenth century involving a pleasure party undertaking an excursion to a specific beauty spot to eat outdoors. Prior to this time picnicking was held inside public rooms and was not associated with rural living. More people have surplus leisure and income and want to enjoy hilltops and the wild. The key transformation from inside to outdoors may well have partly stemmed from Wordsworth's *The Prelude*, reinforced in subsequent poems, such as *The Excursion*, where he connects his awakening consciousness with the landscape and eating outdoors. The Romantics, although concerned with the cognitive processes of perception, memory, judgment and reasoning, set a vogue for walking that was fuelled by guidebooks and institutionalized by anti-enclosure associations, open spaces and footpath societies and linked to the making of the self. The Wordsworths took food with them on their walks from 1800 onwards as seen in Dorothy's Grasmere *Journals*. Picnicking outdoors is specifically English, involves walking and selecting with whom one eats as well as someone preparing and transporting provisions, and connects the participants with the land and its history. It is about choice. Choosing how to spend surplus income and what to eat, where and with whom. It is also about poorer individuals, as *Emma* shows, gaining access to beautiful scenery and views, without having to own the land. Crucially we can also say that this new activity is not linked to hunting or shooting. Jane Austen shows how the picnic can change individuals. Emma leaves the picnic questioning herself and this ultimately leads to her falling in love with Knightley. *Emma* thus draws upon, and over time through the picnic scene, helps develop a specific ethical Englishness that links eating outdoors with an aesthetic standard and way of life.

It was the opening of the London to Portsmouth railway line in 1859 that opened up the enticing possibility to more professional people of living in the Surrey hills, with their wide views, wholesome air and alluring wilderness. Villages, such as Haslemere, Beacon Hill, Grayshott, Hindhead and Guildford, became the focus of a great influx of late Victorian poets, novelists and intellectuals. It was in this wild part of south east England that the likes of Alfred Tennyson, Christina Rossetti, George Eliot, William Allingham, Arthur Conan Doyle, H.G. Wells, Margaret Oliphant, George Bernard Shaw, Flora Thompson, Mrs. Humphrey Ward and dozens of less well-known figures settled.

George Meredith was so captivated by Box Hill that he bought Flint Cottage in the village, where he lived from 1867 until his death in 1909. He immersed himself into the place, walking the hill, 'as its flower, its bird, its prophet.' When I was at university Meredith was remembered as a novelist and his novels, such as *Diana of the Crossways* were regularly dramatized on BBC Radio Four. I had no idea that in his time he was primarily known as a poet and most famous for a sonnet sequence *Modern Love, and Poems of the English Roadside* (1862). Meredith's first wife, the daughter of Thomas Love Peacock, Mary Ellen Nicholls, had left him for the Pre-Raphaelite artist, Henry Wallis, who famously painted Meredith as Chatterton in his 'The Death of Chatterton.'

> By this he knew she wept with waking eyes:
> That, at his hand's light quiver by her head,
> The strange low sobs that shook their common bed

Written from the man's perspective, *Modern Love* concerns a loveless marriage, the problem and difficulties of divorce, and the morality of extramarital sex. It showed that love could die and that both partners had sexual needs and was consequently seen as a shocking exposure of deceit, hate and confusion.

As we admired the panoramic views, comparable to our own Bulbarrow Hill, on a cloudy afternoon and I mentioned *Modern Love*, Leon asked how I became involved with Louise. In common with many others, we first met online. Social networking and Internet dating sites have altered the way we converse about and conduct our relationships. Whilst it is possible to flirt online it can never be the same as meeting face to face and exploring through nonverbal communication. I recalled that an old school friend of ours,

Brent, had been reunited with a former girlfriend online. They rekindled their love and chose to set up a home together thirty years after their first affair. Brent and Gill are still together. Louise has enlivened and enriched my life and there is not a day that goes by when I am not grateful to her for entering my life. Louise pursued and seduced me with charm and wit at a time when I was unhappy and wanted fresh challenges. One advantage of the Internet is that you can probe someone before you meet in order to ascertain whether it is worth pursuing a relationship. Louise and I interrogated one another with subtle and challenging questions. To our astonishment we soon realized that we had considerable compatibility, desire and shared objectives. We made each other laugh, fell passionately in love and committed to one another as soon as we met. The stars had aligned for us to connect, meet and fall in love. We were though subsequently beset by a series of delays and difficulties. Such adversity made us stronger. Life does not always go the way that you would wish and hope for.

The natural world of the Surrey hills penetrates Meredith's philosophical novels and poetry. It was *Poems and Lyrics of the Joy of Earth* (1883) and *A Reading of Earth* (1888) that Thomas venerated. His reading of the poetry is fascinating. He sees the poetry as more than distinct, living observations of English country life and equates it to that of Wordsworth and Shelley in a searing vindication of Meredith's joy in living on the earth. He sees Meredith as 'one of the manliest and deepest of earth's lovers who have written books.' He distinguishes between love of nature and love of earth. For Meredith, love of the earth allows men to become 'warriors in accord / With life to serve.' Love of earth meant breadth, perspective, proportion and thus humour. It is laughter, at our own shortcomings, that allows the earth to revive and flourish again. Meredith reads the natural world in order to understand man. His kinship with the earth allows him to 'look at lesser passing things with a smile, yet without disdain,' and to defend the earth as an animal careless of death. He highlights the stanza from the poem, 'The Lark Ascending,' that includes the lines: 'Our wisdom speaks from failing blood, / Our passion is too full in flood.' His earth poetry has 'sensuousness and vigour, both bodily and intellectual' and his 'Love in the Valley' is the most English of love poems. Thomas concludes by seeing Meredith as not so much an admirer and lover of nature but 'a part of her, one of her most splendid creatures, fit to be ranked with the whitebeam and the lark, and the south-west wind,' in a sentence that gloriously echoes Meredith's own subjects.

The connections with Wordsworth are clear in the sense that Meredith is concerned with living and walking the earth. Meredith organized walking tours around Box Hill and became something of a guru figure to Robert Louis Stevenson, Conan Doyle, J.M. Barrie, Max Beerbohm, George Gissing, Henry James and various statesmen. He was deeply Darwinian and his idea of the earth feeds into our concept of Englishness by extolling the living and the enduring scenery of the English countryside. However, Meredith's poetry, despite dealing primarily with love and our relationship with the earth, has not been part of the academic reading of 'ecopoetry' nor gained the public awareness that Thomas hoped for. He is perhaps more of a writer's writer, whose work has had a hidden impact. Had he been as radical in his life and thought as Shelley, for example, he perhaps might be seen in a different light. As Oscar Wilde wrote of Meredith: 'His style is chaos illumined by flashes of lightning.' He left Flint Cottage to the National Trust, an organisation that stems from the impact of the Romantics, for them to keep in trust in perpetuity. They leased the house, worth £1.35 million, a few years ago and it is no longer open to the public. However, he set the trend and others left their local homes to the National Trust in an effort to preserve and safeguard the area's beauty. Meredith remains an unusual and largely forgotten Victorian, despite having written the poem whose setting to music has become the personification of Englishness. He remains at an unusual angle to Englishness and the kind of amnesia associated with him and other radical and humanitarian figures is at the root of my journey.

Chapter Six

The Lark Ascending

As an increasingly overcast light descended I rued my bad
timing to be cycling along the Epsom Road bypassing
Dorking, during Drive Time. I am not a particularly practical
person. Homeward bound cars whizzed and whooshed by at
speed along the narrow road. It was not a great experience.
Despite the woeful signage, I knew that a right hand turning
would lead to the A25 or A246 and the road that Thomas had
cycled towards Guildford. Although I seriously confused my
left and right hand during my only driving test, I have been
blessed with an innate sense of direction. I don't really benefit
from looking for the sun or map reading so much as using
my memory and if I haven't been there before, as in this case,
I orientate my body to the north and south and thus to the
required direction. I love old maps but find them almost
redundant in terms of the sixth sense. I thus managed to find
myself cycling through Westcott Heath past Rookery Wood
and looking out for Deerleap Wood on the right.

I had opted out of cycling through Dorking and finding any
of the buildings associated with that colossus of twentieth
century music, Ralph Vaughan Williams (1872-1958). The
composer of *The Lark Ascending* had lived and composed
much of his music in and around Dorking and Box Hill. In
many ways *The Lark Ascending*, based on Meredith's *Poems and
Lyrics of the Joy of Earth* (1883), stems from the same earth and
sensibilities as *In Pursuit of Spring* and Thomas' poetry.

Composed in 1914, *The Lark Ascending* has a gentle, seemingly untroubled lyricism that captures a peaceful past that issues a hovering flight over a semi-industrial scene that many now see as nostalgic. The intention of the poem and composition is to instil a love and joy in the natural world, with the Surrey hills and woodland being the locus of this, through the lark. The poem situates labouring men,

> Whose lives, by many a battle-dint
> Defaced, and grinding wheels on flint,
> Yield substance, though they sing not, sweet

as producing nourishment through the earth with only a hint of disenchantment. The overriding sense from the poem is that the lark, its flight and song, has spiritual significance in relation to those that work the land. It absorbs in its 'brain's reflex' the substance and song of those with deep love of the earth. This is the meaning that excited both Thomas and the composer. From his readings of Jefferies, Vaughan Williams would surely have seen the lark as emblematic of a disappearing culture and it is this element that is grasped as signifying Englishness. Another element stems from the music itself, which employs low chords at the beginning, the parallel motions of ancient music found in folk songs and holy music, expanding with the wings of the lark to higher chords. It is this that listeners recognise as old England with its ancient harmonies and embedded simplicity. Incredibly difficult to play, the piece topped the all-time classic music charts from 2007-2010 and remains immensely popular.

However, Vaughan Williams was more complex than this early piece. I first came across his arrangements and compositions for the *English Hymnal* (1906) at school. His work in that area greatly contributed to the Church of England and enriched our heritage. Yet he was an agnostic radical far more concerned with the spiritual journey than theological overtones. Follow his music from the Whitmanesque *A Sea Symphony* (1910), his settings of George Herbert's *Five Mystical Songs* (1911) through to the *Fourth Symphony* (1935), *The Pilgrim's Progress* opera of 1951 and beyond. The music critics did not welcome Vaughan Williams' mixture of folksong, hymnal and mystical in the 1910s. *The Times* reviewer noted of the *Fantasia On A Theme From Tallis* 'One is living in two centuries at once...' In contrast, the young poet and composer, Ivor Gurney, left the premiere in a state of disturbance and bewilderment and spent the night walking the streets of Gloucester unable to sleep and fired with excitement.

Vaughan Williams' music is often called the apotheosis of Englishness. It is the pastoral in his music that is being linked to a place, an almost mythical England. Yet it is not mythical. It is here on the old London road, in the richest part of the country, where the real relations of the land are usurped by nostalgic memories and emotions of a languid tranquility, where Meredith imbibed the flight and song of birds. As I write this I can hear Leon reminding me that the area may contain the some of the most expensive houses in the country but it also contains some of the poorest and most forgotten of our rural poor.

The Lark Ascending and *Fantasia On A Theme From Tallis* mark a time and place of English identity. They are linked to nationalism and the collecting of folk songs at the turn of the last century. I tend to see composers, such as Vaughan Williams, Percy Grainger, Gustav Holst, Frederick Delius and George Butterworth as finding an English alternative to dominant European styles and simply trying to earn a living. In 1906 the Board of Education formally allowed the teaching of folk songs in schools. There was a new market that stemmed from the belief that the Empire was coming under threat. These, though, were strongly socialist, internationalist, vegetarian, earth loving composers that looked to poetry for vision and collected folk songs to incorporate into their compositions.

Vaughan Williams was an agnostic radical, a progressive that was part of the Socialist Society that met at William Morris' home at Hammersmith. Here he heard lectures by George Bernard Shaw, H.G. Wells, Eleanor Marx, Edward Carpenter and rubbed shoulders with W.B. Yeats, Oscar Wilde, Cecil Sharp, George Trevelyan, Henry Salt and so on. Theirs was an ethical, poetic socialism. They were concerned with poetry, music and how people lived as much as with living conditions, workers' rights and female suffrage. As a group they were looking backward to older societies and forward to idealised or dying ones. This is seen in Morris's *News From Nowhere* (1890), set in the future when England is transmuted into a medieval earthly paradise, Richard Jefferies' *After London, or Wild England* (1885), which reclaims London as a wilderness after a natural disaster and H.G. Wells' *The Time Machine* (1895), which sees social and industrial degeneration leading to a future dying Earth. Vaughan Williams set Blake's *Book of Job*, with a libretto by the neo-pagan, Geoffrey Keynes, resplendent with aggressive syncopations to signify Satan and Hell, and that of Walt Whitman to music. It is Whitman's poetry with its structural and metrical freedom, spiritual intensity that helps to liberate Vaughan Williams musical imagination and he seems to have learned as much from Maurice Ravel in Paris as from Sir Hubert Parry's insistence upon studying Tudor and Elizabethan choral music. This situates his music of place in a less nationalistic context. It is this background and quality that has been lost in readings of Vaughan Williams and the English Folk Revival. The argument that the folk song collectors appropriated songs to make them politically and educational acceptable and thus reduce their challenge to authority and the class structure is an erroneous one. The originals were found, saved and notated. They can still be enlivened and made relevant by the likes of the Unthanks, Eliza Carthy or Chris Wood. They remain part of our cultural and political heritage.

Deerleap Wood occupied the hollow land between the rising road and Downs, running parallel to the road and grabbed Thomas' attention with its oaks and their accumulated 'purplish' branch work. It is now some distance from the road that Thomas cycled and surrounded by 'Private' signs. Thomas writes about having a choice of lanes to Guildford and it strikes me that the world is diminished by the current lack of choice. It may be simpler and easier but it is surely duller. As I needed a break from cycling I decided to walk for a while and catch my breath in the Wood. I found a way in near a memorial to Samuel Wilberforce, the son of William, the anti-slavery campaigner, and found a Bronze Age bell barrow nearby covered in saplings. The wood was beginning to lose its winter stillness. I missed the yellow of a dandelion or celandine. Primroses, catkins, sallow were not enough in an overcast light. I felt the melancholy of a wood without much character. I was disappointed. It struck me that the landowners, by denying public access to the Wood and covering the monument, were somewhat out of touch with English heritage thinking as well as unappreciative of all the Wood's needs. Disappointed and deflated, my thoughts turned to what constitutes and who decides what is an authentic English identity. Woodland life and birdsong are such deeply held English identities that to deny access is thoroughly un-English.

Cycling on and returning to more urban surroundings I reflected on the global village of multi-ethnic Englishness and those that run counter to such landowners. I immediately thought of The Imagined Village, a musical collaboration started in Dorset in 2004, and the widening ethnic diversity and different languages of contemporary England. I heard the distinct tones of the Anglo-Caribbean, the Asian, the Thai brides, Turkish, Iraqi and Afghani and more recent Polish, Russian and Latvian. Named after Georgina Boyes' academic book attacking the English Folk Revival for being phoney, The Imagined Village's fusion of multicultural world roots and English traditional folk embrace the wit of Martin Carthy, the Asian dub of Transglobal Underground and the Afro Celtic Sound System. Seeing them live is a feast for the ears and eyes. Sheema Mukherjee absorbed North Indian classical music and the western tradition side-by-side and is a formidable musician contributing cascading sitar sounds and funky improvisation. Her composition, 'Bending The Dark,' developed for the 2012 Cultural Olympiad, integrates their distinctive ethnic music into an extended musical rendering of second-generation immigrant experience. The twin fiddle playing singers, Eliza Carthy and Jackie Oates, contribute texture and found material. Star turn, Sikh percussionist, Johnny Kalsi, has an infectious enthusiasm that adds another vibrant element to the heady mix. The whole ensemble is a thoughtful and tongue-in-cheek continuation of the ethical socialist stance of English folk music that was sparked by Cecil Sharp and Vaughan Williams. It is the informed musician / poet sticking one finger up to the critic and I love it!

The academics that have attacked Sharp and Vaughan Williams for appropriating songs from the rural poor for their own ends have no song theory and fail to see that notating and recording such a song is an act of reclamation and creates access irrespective of class position and any subsequent alterations. A song, composition or poem is never a fixed entity. It is mutable and can be re-interpreted and transformed. As the historian E.P. Thompson pointed out, it is more a matter of re-examining the original, asking new questions and seeking to recover any lost customs and beliefs that informed them. I am reminded of the poet, Irina Ratushinskaya's comment to me that she wanted to write a poem that everyone knew but no one knew the author's name. Moreover, if a song has substance it can be and should be both preserved, adapted and extended, as in the example of the traditional song 'Bushes and Briars.' Vaughan Williams heard this being sung by Charles Potipher in Brentwood, Essex in December 1905 and wrote it down, with its possible variants. Since then male and female singers have performed it, most famously by Julie Christie in the 1967 film *Far From The Madding Crowd*, and a male chorus. Its origins are unknown. It has also been referenced contextually by Sandy Denny's 1972 song of the same name that brings into question the pastoral and spiritual and forces the listener to consider the impact of Vaughan Williams' work. It is the role of art to probe and question.

Indeed, The Invisible Village member Chris Wood's analysis of our current malaise and unrest over immigration in terms of national identity is particularly cogent. He argues that the English have a legacy left to us by Anon in terms of songs, tunes, dances, ceremony, custom, lore, vocabulary, craft, magic and an instinctive understanding of the pedagogical power of narrative that is too apposite to ignore. He sees our cultural uncertainty as stemming from Empire, two World Wars, a limiting class structure and the long shadow of the perceived cultural confidence of America and our European neighbours and dates this back to our cultural dispersal following the enclosure acts. He contrasts the 'official' versions of our history with the treasure chest of Anon that offers a sublime vision of English life and opinion and can teach the English to love themselves. Wood is compelled by a desire to see beneath political correctness and cultural reticence to find the best words to give our inheritance its fullest and richest expression. This is encapsulated in his emphasis on the second part of the second commandment to 'Love thy neighbor as you would love yourself.' His 2005 album before his fame spread outside the folk music scene was entitled *The Lark Descending*. He is in touch with our dissenting traditions, writes about injustices and seeks constructive ways out of our Imperial past. Being aware of our historical and literary past and Anon, as Thomas and Vaughan Williams showed, enables writers and composers to draw upon and / or adapt for contemporary relevance an enlivening and enriching heritage. Wood is a proud English singer in the radical Wordsworthian tradition of troubadours and concerned to show the English how to love themselves, have more fun and to refuse ghettoization.

When I think of the history of England and Englishness, I see a blending of cultures, socially, genetically and historically and that the established Church has always had to become pluralistic in order to survive. The Protestant Church firstly accepted the Jews, then the Catholics, French Huguenots, Quakers and Baptists. After the Civil War, religious dissent was enacted in the Act of Toleration (1702). The English have full-scale religious freedom that ranges from atheism to allowing extreme Muslim fundamentalists to promulgate the end of such freedom. This religious tolerance, stemming from the pressure of the Dissenting tradition more than the Church of England's hierarchy, later embraced Hinduism, Buddhism and from the Sixties the diversity of New Age thinking and beliefs. Its transplant in Boston with the Pilgrim Fathers and other dissenters is perhaps its most glorious and diverse offspring. This broad Church of thinking over time has given the English a love of toleration and acceptance of difference. It is one of the reasons why so many different races want to live here. We are a sanctuary for the world and should be proud as such. Yes, big business is happy to have cheap labour but that is only one part of a wider and deeper picture that is rooted in our Imperial past. Our elite is a mongrel with tentacles in different faiths and ancestry.

Whereas Thomas could take shortcuts and encountered walkers that he sees in an almost hallucinogenic manner, I was forced to cycle on one road. His chosen lane was peopled by 'genial muscular Christians with their daughters,' 'genially muscular agnostics with no children,' 'bands of scientifically-minded ramblers with knickerbockers, spectacles, and cameras; a trio of young chaps singing their way to a pub; one or two solitaries going at five miles an hour with or without hats.' These and other rural walkers, described in some detail, gave Thomas a feeling that he had been 'forestalled (to put it mildly).' It is another of those strange paragraphs that raise more questions than can be answered. Why do these figures delay him? How small was the lane? Surely he stopped and spoke to them? I can say that the modern cyclist has no time to observe other travellers. It is a matter of concentrating on the road, traffic ahead, to the side and behind. I saw and heard birds far more than people as I cycled through Abinger Hammer. There was no sign of the stream or pond that Thomas mentions. The woodland survives and it was from there that I took sustenance from the sound and presence of birds. I was hoping to hear a nightingale. Rooks cawed and cars hissed instead. As Shelley wrote: 'A poet is a nightingale who sits in darkness and sings to cheer its own solitude with sweet sounds.'

Unlike Thomas, I decided to cycle off the A25 and look at 'the prettiest village in Surrey.' The visionary painter, William Hyde (1857-1925), in the tradition of Samuel Palmer, and his potter wife, Kate, lived at Shere from 1895 and developed his bleak pastoral vision amongst the Surrey Hills. He illustrated Meredith's *Nature Poems* and *The Poetical Works of John Milton* (1904). His wind-blown trees and stormy clouds prefigure future destruction. He was also something of a symbolist decorating his illustrations with full-breasted nymphs and owls. Despite his connections with the Garnetts and Ford Madox Ford, he remained an outsider figure and has only recently been re-discovered. Shere is idyllic and was featured in D.W. Griffith's 1918 silent film, *Hearts of the World*, Powell and Pressburger's 1946 masterpiece *A Matter of Life and Death*, as Reeve's village, and more recently in *Bridget Jones: The Edge of Reason* and other films. Suddenly, flowing through the centre of the village was the Tillingbourne stream that Thomas mentions.

Shere is mentioned in the Domesday Book and has a Norman church, narrow streets and extraordinary number of well-preserved National Heritage cottages. I was thirsty and needed a pint. I wasn't used to the antiseptic streets and total absence of a feral underclass. I chose The White Horse over the Edwardian William Bray pub, as it looked more like an old time pub than a restaurant. The White Horse did not disappoint, although service was slow and the man that served me knew nothing about the pub's history. I decided to sit on a bench at the front of the pub and observe the comings and goings. I checked messages. Nothing. I drank another pint and calculated that I would be entering

76

Guildford within twenty minutes. I cycled out of Shere with the sound of low melodious whistles interspersed with gunfire echoing in my head.

Chapter Seven

Englishness

Englishness is a cultural identity, derived from and evolving since the Angles, Saxons and Jutes that emigrated from Denmark and northern Germany inhabited England. It involves a sense of history, a commitment and belonging to a dwelling-place and a love of the English language and its usage. It also involves an unwritten code of behavior. It is not to be confused with the conflicting versions of being English or British provided by nationalists, racists and politicians. It is rather a deeper definition that is understood by a French woman or an African and one that is socially historically determined. This underlying historical and cultural identity, derived from our literature, ranges across boundaries and is constantly shifting, albeit slowly, as the language, literature and voices of England changes.

England has been multicultural and multiethnic for some time and our older Imperial notions of Englishness that involved a certain sense of racial superiority; masculinity and notions of gentlemanly behavior have been deeply eroded. Englishness has become a more fluid and open identity, albeit under threat from those that do not believe in difference, tolerance and openness, and based much more upon place and behaviour than class, ethnicity or gender. It is an attitude of mind. Anxiety over what it means to be English seems to have been a continual concern. Daniel Defoe's 1701 anti-Tory satire, *The True-Born Englishman*, shows a worry that Englishness was being diluted. Recent Mori opinion polls suggest that English people do not know whether their allegiance lies with the U.K, England, their geographical region or immediate local community. There is also a strong sense that we are losing our distinctiveness to an homogeneity that some say derives from the deeper effects of corporate business, as exemplified by Tesco and other global businesses, that want to limit and control consumer choice by positioning themselves outside town and city centres.

I tend to relate this homogeneity with its limited range of building usage and its resemblance to the cities of the old Soviet bloc to a lack of architectural, civic and cultural vision and plain old corruption. Guildford grew from a market town into a city as a result of the Wey canal, opened in 1653, the cloth industry and later as a coaching, road and railway terminus for London and the south coast. Poorly situated departmental stores, shopping centres and a multi-storey car park have spoilt the historic centre. The narrow cobbled High Street retains some character with its Elizabethan Guildhall clock and there is a sense of a living and active town albeit lacking the Georgian buildings and heritage of Bath.

I appreciated and applaud the cycleways of Guildford and was beginning to understand why Thomas mentions pubs so much on his journey. As it was beginning to drizzle, I was able to stop safely and put on my waterproofs. The more I cycled the more I looked forward to rehydrating and looked out for pubs, as Thomas did. I see pubs as a link to our past and in need of support in terms of bringing the community together. I arrived wet and slightly bedraggled and couldn't remember where Thomas stayed. He mentions seeing a motorcar and the rain. I later read that it was a commercial temperance hotel and that he was desperate to drink tea. After supper he went for a 'haphazard' walk to the Miller's Arms, at Mill Lane, past the waterworks and on to the 'faintly nautical cottages' that looked over a gas-lit space at the river and The Britannia pub at Mill Mead. He is absorbed by the dark water, the dark houses, the silvered, wet, moonlit streets and at corners a young man, or two young men talking to a girl. He is not in the mood for conversation. It is spare, desolate description.

Of the pubs that Thomas mentions, only The Britannia survives. Thomas noted the signs at pubs that welcomed cyclists. The Cyclists' Touring Club, (CTC) the UK's largest cycling charity, whose Patron is H.M. the Queen and President, Channel Four newscaster, Jon Snow, is based at Railton Road, where it publishes *Cycle* magazine, providing expert advice and support for cyclists. Founded in 1878 as the Bicycle Touring Club and subsequently re-named the organization has its origins in the early days of cycling when the bicycle opened up new horizons for independent travel. In 1936 it created a cycling proficiency scheme that was adopted nationally in 1948 and I recall taking as a ten year old on my first bicycle. The organization, which has 70,000 members, continues to campaign for cycle training, better road safety and to protect cyclists' interests. It has a Challenge for Change Workplace Cycle Challenge to get more people to cycle to work that is successfully converting non-cyclists into occasional cyclists and occasional cyclists into regular cyclists. Indeed, my employers have joined the 'Cycle to Work' Scheme thanks to our Bursar being an enthusiastic cyclist and more employees are cycling to work than ever before. As I had not booked a room on this occasion, it took some phone calls with some grumpy and unfriendly receptionists before I found a hotel willing to accept my bicycle and myself, albeit at a price. We need hotels to put those 'Cyclists Welcome' signs back up.

That evening I recalled an earlier visit to Guildford when I had given a poetry reading at the University, been given a superb meal and spent the night drinking red wine and making love with an old flame in the halls of residence. A more recent visit to read at the Boileroom, an alternative music venue, in Stoke Fields, had been pleasant but I had ended up staying overnight in a room with a hole in the wall and vowed never again. At breakfast, in the morning I met a sad looking bearded backpacker from Yorkshire, who was intent on walking to Cornwall. He had bowel cancer for the second time, had left his wife and young daughter to become a walker and had lost his phone charger. I let him use my phone and he seemed genuinely happy. He had refused more chemotherapy and was putting his faith in the walking cure. He had always dreamed of walking to Cornwall and wanted a journey of discovery. He said that he was on 'the road less travelled,' which was not a misattribution of Robert Frost's famous poem, but rather a psychological and spiritual discipline involving enjoying the mystery of existence and beauty of nature on the road. He said that he was looking for true community. I told him that Guildford was possibly not a likely candidate and that any road south was a better option. He smiled. I read him Louise's update: 'So every morning when I step outside, someone wolf whistles at me, and it's kinda nice and I walk differently and stick my chest out and flick my hair back and smile...seductively. Until today, when I discovered where the whistles emanate from: The neighbour's pet parrot.' He smiled again and said 'Love is as love does.' We finished our coffees and wished each other good luck on our respective journeys.

Civic Guildford barely acknowledges let alone recognizes one of its more interesting literary figures. That cultural amnesia is one of the motivations in undertaking this journey. We are forgetting where we come from and those people that made the English such a vital, tolerant and progressive people. We are forgetting our love of eccentricity.

Edward Carpenter (1844-1929) was a poet, anthologist, pioneering socialist and radical humanitarian who lived in Guildford from 1922 until his death. Raised from the stock market riches of his father in Brighton and educated at Trinity Hall, Cambridge, he gave up being a curate in 1874 to lecture and write. Inspired by Walt Whitman's poetry, he wrote the epic poem cycle *Towards Democracy* (1883) and made the connection between his own homosexuality and democratic politics. He became enthused by the need to provide education for the working class and moved to Leeds and became involved in radical politics. A lectureship with the University Extension took him to Sheffield where, in between encounters with railway men, porters, clerks, signalmen, ironworkers he discovered south Yorkshire's sturdier brand of socialism, in contrast to the decadent affluence of Brighton and Cambridge. It was here that he wrote the socialist marching song, 'England Arise!' He went to India and returned inspired by Eastern mysticism, Hinduism, yoga, sandals and *The Bhagavad-Gita*. He became a prophet of a new age of fellowship in which social relations would be transformed by a new spiritual consciousness.

Carpenter advocated homosexual equality, women's rights, prison reform, free love, recycling, nudism and started a co-operative farm in the Cordwell Valley, near Sheffield in order to put his beliefs into practice. His ethical socialism was not concerned with wage levels and working conditions so much as a philosophy and way of life that would enhance both men and women. He drew upon Platonic tradition, German idealism, Hinduism and Shelley to advocate new forms of associating and relating, a new aesthetic of the everyday in harmony with nature. Known as the English Thoreau, he was a founding member of the Independent Labour Party, the Fabian Society and other socialist and humanitarian societies. He defied late Victorian morality by living with his working class lover, George Merrill, from 1898 until Merrill's death. They were visited by E.M. Forster and inspired his posthumously published novel, *Maurice*. This in turn was read in manuscript by D.H. Lawrence, giving him the freedom to be more sexually frank and inspired *Lady Chatterley's Lover*, his heterosexual version of *Maurice*. Carpenter's circle of friends included Whitman, Rabindranath Tagore, William Morris, Oscar Wilde, George Bernard Shaw, Henry and Kate Salt, Havelock and Edith Ellis, Robert Graves, E.M. Forster, Isadora Duncan, Olive Schreiner, Annie Besant and countless less well-known figures. He was the target of George Orwell's attack in *The Road To Wigan Pier* on 'every fruit-juice drinker, nudist, sandal-wearer, sex-maniac, Quaker, pacifist and feminist in England.'

Carpenter bridges the gap between the narrow-minded late Victorians and more emotionally open and liberal moderns. He was an archetypal sandal-wearing yoga-loving vegetarian that could also be a template for Edward Thomas' the Other Man. His attempt to add the spiritual to party politics sticks out in contrast to our recent experiences of unethical and morally corrupt politicians. This allied to his broad humanitarianism helping lay the foundations for homosexual and women's rights make him worthy of memory. He is not mentioned in civic Guilford's literary connections and that cultural amnesia needs some consideration.

My friend, Sarah Connor, put me on to a book that offers a speculative reading of our tendency for mechanistic thinking and consequent amnesia towards the non-conformist visionaries and democrats that forged our history. Iain McGilchrist's *The Master and his Emissary: The Divided Brain and the Making of the Western World* (2009). This groundbreaking book argues that the left and right hemispheres of the brain have differing insights, values and priorities. Based on a considerable body of extensive research, McGilchrist argues that each side has a distinct 'take' on the world. The right hemisphere sees itself as connected to the world, whereas the left stands aloof from it. This has affected our understanding of language and reason, music and time as well as all living things and the world in which we live. The left hemisphere, with its mechanistic approach, alienated from the living world, has grabbed power and produced a rigidity obsessed with bureaucratic structure and narrow self-interest at the expense of vision, happiness and alternative possibilities. Whilst I am unable to comment upon McGilchrist's reading of functional brain neuroscience, I can say that other neuroscientists broadly support his position and that the cultural implications of his discoveries are huge.

In McGilchrist's terms right side thinking knows no boundaries, does not perceive of itself as separate, but is expansive, concerned with the living, close to nature with a circular view of the world. Left side thinking, in contrast, is more linear and methodical, occupied with the past and future, in a cold and calculating intelligence, defining itself as separate from the rest of the world. This wonderfully stimulating book supports my contention that the English collectively have forgotten the art of lateral thinking and accepted an alienating, sub-standard way of life that our poets, artists, visionaries, non-conformists, inventors and experimental scientists have worked towards transcending and transforming.

As I began my ride to the Hog's Back and Farnham that morning my mind turned to how Thomas' journey helped develop our understanding and appreciation of Englishness. I felt as if I was on a mission. The Hog's Back is a narrow ridge, 150 metres / 500 feet above sea level, over the North Downs. It is part of the ancient ridgeway from Wiltshire to Kent and now part of the A31 with a dual carriageway and hardly any of the views that Jane Austen wrote so admiringly of in a letter to her sister, Cassandra, in May 1813 when she travelled along the Hog's Back. I soon felt that I was cycling in the wrong place. It was a busy and fast road and I didn't want to stop and look for an alternative route. I felt the cold that morning and was pleased to be wearing gloves. I wanted to cycle at speed and warm up. I arrived at Farnham in fifty minutes.

The idea of Englishness, at heart, embraces predominantly rural imagery such as the village cricket green, thatched cottages, the pub, the cream teas, hills and woodlands and is intimately tied to the pastoral and is based more on the England of the Nineteen Sixties or Seventies than 2012. It is imbued in such sayings as 'It's just not cricket,' meaning that there is an absence of fair play. Cricket is distinctly English and its attitude towards time has an historical root. Cricket provides an example of how Englishness is worked out in social interaction. Englishness works through the appreciation of its unwritten codes of behaviour. Cricket involves taking the long view and adapting to changing conditions over days. Observation of the weather is a pre-requisite. It involves playing by rules. The boundary of Englishness in cricket is contained within the concept of the no-ball, the arguments for and against the front foot and back foot rules, and the rules of appeal.

Englishness involves tolerance and respect for difference and the other as well as the constitutional monarchy, with its ritualized institutions and music. It has a built in nostalgia for a bygone period and is continually being modified as we challenge and change our written and unwritten rules. That music, for example, composed at the beginning of Imperial decline, draws upon arrangements of our greatest poets, such as Milton and Blake, and has remained fairly constant for a century. The English love of poetry since the Tudors and Stuarts, so intimately connected with our language development and of our 'green and pleasant land' has remained a powerful pull on our self-understanding. Englishness, at base, comes from our education, media and walking the hills and woodland. It comes from our greatest poets and writers and filters through the population. It is also an attitude of mind that encompasses many attitudes that are not always employed at the right times. The English are never fully organized or prepared and unlike the French, Dutch or Italians, for example, have no concept of an agreed compromise. Our balance has been affected by the continuing class system and a failure to understand civic responsibility, especially of the voluntary kind. People working voluntarily for the common good have been truncated by bureaucracy and simpleton health and safety regulations. Whenever he expected dangerous ice, one of our neighbours would rise early to grit the roads. He was never paid and did this as his contribution to our wellbeing. He felt that he was giving back to the community. When snowdrifts blocked the local roads, he would use his plough to clear the roads. Mr. Lane has sadly died and this activity has been hounded out. Farmers are now severely restricted in how they can help the community during crisis times. Meanwhile, our local council is unable to cope with ice and snow for week after week. This illustrates the dominance of left-side thinking over right-side thinking.

The old Hegelian approach of thesis, anti-thesis and synthesis has never taken hold. In contrast, the English are often set in an either / or dualism that encumbers government policy and invariably leaves half the country disenchanted. A typical example would be the Winchester by-pass and the loss of Twyford Down in 1994. A new by-pass was required and there was direct action against the proposed loss of ancient chalk downland. The either / or thinking dominated the Department of Environment and the third way of a tunnel, which would have appeased both viewpoints and save the hillside, was barely mentioned. It is as if the English cannot take that other step. Our European neighbours, in contrast, have less trouble in acquiescing to a workable compromise. They also know that we have our faults and quaint customs, such as cricket and tea drinking, and our monarchy and a range of eccentrics, that make us quite distinct.

One possible reason that the English do not possess that turn of mind that moves beyond dualistic thinking is that in the nineteenth century the English produced great essayists and novelists rather than philosophers. The nearest English equivalent to Hegel was perhaps William Hazlitt, who is sadly a forgotten figure, and we have to wait until John Ruskin much later in the century for a thinker of similar standing. In between it is the Romantic poets and our novelists from Dickens, Mrs. Gaskell, Disraeli, George Eliot, Hardy, D.H. Lawrence through to E.M. Forster and Virginia Woolf that dominate the condition of England thinking. Lawrence in *Lady Chatterley's Lover* noted that industrial England was blotting agricultural England and that a new England was blotting out old England not in an organic but mechanical way. More recent writers and cultural commentators from Orwell through John Betjeman to Julian Barnes in his novel,

England, England (1998) and Jeremy Paxman have produced lists in order to define Englishness. This tells us more about the English mind than Englishness per se. Englishness is much more an attitude of mind and behaviour than an empirical list, notwithstanding the magisterial listing of the annual *Wisden Cricketer's Almanack* and the daily Social Register published in the *Times* newspaper.

Either / or dualistic thinking has a decontextualized view of the world. It is a kind of imprisoned logic in a single plane of vision that omits our connection to place, locality, the earth and our involvement in a community. The attachment to roots, place and ecology that one finds in Shakespeare, Blake, Wordsworth and Shelley has been increasingly sidelined by mechanistic thinking, policy making and unethical business and banking practices underpinned by belief in linear progress that is vehemently anti-community and anti-local. Amongst the biggest villains have been the supermarket chains, who are responsible for the loss of so many of our pubs, the bankers, and the politicians that gave up our local food producing markets for short-term gains elsewhere. Fortunately some small food producers are finding ways of avoiding the dominance of the supermarkets through alternative marketing on online communities, supported by the hub in the community projects, farmers markets and are rebuilding local markets for home produce that have been taken away. One of the people most supportive and concerned in this area is H.R.H. The Prince of Wales. Indeed, Prince Charles supported our local village shop, through a Royal visit with the Duchess of Cornwall, when it was re-opened in The White Horse. The landlord, Chris Sargent has made the pub the hub of village life and believes the shop, post office, pub and view of the woodland from the church are at the heart of Englishness. His youngest son, Ben is a patriotic Englishman. In his early twenties he rises from his seat whenever the national anthem is played, even at the start of the Eurovision Song Contest!! Such patriotism is rare. I am reminded of Johnny Speight's comic character, Alf Garnett, beautifully played by Warren Mitchell, standing whenever the anthem was played and looking askance at his Scouse son-in-law who remained seated. For Chris, the pub is at the heart of Englishness and, as he says, Englishness can be observed in a pub. Chris, who has been a great help in discussing this book's themes, continues a wonderful family tradition. He was given a copy of Rudyard Kipling's poem, 'If' by his father at the age of sixteen and advised to note its advice. He, in turn, gave copies to his sons when they became sixteen. Chris is an astute, community aware landlord and provides a much needed local focal point. It was outside the White Horse that we met to watch the Olympic flame pass by in July.

The English are incredibly resourceful as Prince Charles has noted and there are always people attempting to think outside of this rigid linearity. Further afield, one thinks of the smartphone and online networking as other examples of intuition side stepping mechanistic thinking to actually aid and transform our local communities. They have been part of the protest movements in Iran and in the Arab Spring uprisings in Tunisia, Egypt, Libya, Yemen, Bahrain, Syria and elsewhere. These devices, with their origins in the San Francisco counter-culture, aided by English ingenuity, have been a democratic source of liberation and continue to give hope that our local communities can be revived and made to work much better.

Chapter Eight

The Pub

In contrast to entering Guildford, cycling off the A31 round the Shepherd and lock roundabout down the by-pass with the grass verge on the left and into Farnham is a joy. I soon found myself on a small lane sedately cycling into Abbey Street and walking across the road towards Costa Coffee in West Street.

Farnham, nestling in the Wey valley, has grown organically evolving through time within a country setting and retains the marks of its history. Originally 'Fearnhamme,' being the ferns by the water meadow, began as a Saxon village built upon a Roman settlement and contains the heart of England in its history. Farnham's seventh century ecclesiastical charter and boundary list shows the Anglo-Saxon roots of the English language in its place-naming with words such as –ham (ham), -ford (ford), -hyth (hythe), -burh (bury), -leah (ley) and –feld (field). The Saxon King Caedwalla gave the village to the Bishop of Winchester, who built the castle in the mid twelfth century, as a convenience for his travels between Winchester and London. Farnham gained its own charter of rights in 1249, gradually gaining more independence over time. In the Tudor period, Farnham prospered thanks to the cloth industry, wheat and hops growing, wheat and pottery production. Queen Elizabeth gave the town a new charter in 1566 and the grammar school opened in 1585. In the seventeenth century, Farnham had the largest corn market in southern England when coastal shipping was hindered by almost continual warfare in the English Channel. The Parliamentarians occupied Farnham Castle during the Civil War (1642-1646). The damaged parts were repaired during the Restoration and the Bishop of Winchester used it as a residence until well into the last century.

The Captain of the Castle garrison was the Spenserian poet and satirist, George Wither, whose *Abuses, Stript and Whipt* (1613), an enormously popular work in the tradition of Piers Plowman, upset both the Court and parliament. Born at Alton, he was something of a maverick, in and out prison for his satires. His *Motto* (1621) sold several thousand copies in official and pirate editions. His *Hymns and Songs of the Church* (1622-23), issued under a patent from King James I, was the first English hymnal. During the Civil War, he initially sided with the Royalists but soon changed sides and raised a troop of horsemen for Parliament and was given Farnham, as he lived under Beacon Hill. After a few days occupation he left the Castle undefended, and marched towards London. His home was plundered, and the Royalists captured him. His life was spared by the intervention of Sir John Denham on the grounds that if Wither lived he could not be possibly the worst poet in England. He turned up at the siege of Gloucester and fought in the battle of Naseby. Things went well until he upset Cromwell. At the Restoration, he was back in the Tower of London for three years and finally became a Quaker.

Hops and the malting of barley succeeded wheat and cloth as the mainstay of the town's prosperity from the 1750s. Hops were grown on the former common fields up to the foot of the Hog's Back, extending some ten miles along the valley. Hop kilns, with their distinctive chimney tops, were built to dry the hops in the town centre. Businesses closed their shops for a week at hop drying time when red herrings were eaten in celebration of the harvest. The hazel and hawthorn quickset hedges and trees planted to protect the hops from the wind added to the area's beauty. Damson trees were planted as a warning against blight in what was a tricky but highly lucrative cultivation. The delicately flavoured beer financed Farnham for the best part of one hundred and fifty years and still continues in a much reduced way.

Farnham hops were once considered the best in England and superior to the Kent hops. Hops, humulus lupulus or 'wolf of the woods,' are named after their cones, as in Long White, Oval, Long Square Garlick, White Bine, Green Bine and so on. In 1750 Peckham Williams began cultivating a White Bine Grape hop from a cutting. This became the famous Farnham White Bine hop, which commanded one third more and sometimes double the price of other hops. There was considerable rivalry with the growers of Kentish hops as William Marshall's *The Rural Economy of the Southern Counties: Comprizing Kent, Surrey, Sussex, The Isle of White, the Chalk Hills of Wiltshire, Hampshire etc, and including the Culture and Management of Hops in the Districts of Maidstone, Canterbury and the Valley of Farnham* (1798) indicates. Marshall favoured the Kentish hops, the Golding, Canterbury and Fuggle, which he claimed produced twice the quantity of bitter and aroma. Eventually, the Farnham White Bine was duplicated in Kent where it was named the Canterbury White Bine and is still grown. The last Farnham White Bine's were grubbed up in

1929 as a result of a severe attack of downy mildew. Farnham is a hard water area and good for beer production. In a nice twist, the Goldings hop from Kent, developed in 1790, is now used by the Hog's Back Brewery, based at Manor Farm, Tongham, in their award-winning T.E.A. (Traditional English Ale). The Hog's Back Brewery has some wonderfully named beers, such as 'Rip Snorter,' 'Santa's Wobble,' 'Still Wobbling,' and 'Wobble in a Bottle.'

Until the 1850s brewing in the Wey valley was a localized affair, with many of the inns brewing their own ales. Wealthy householders and farmers brewed primarily for their own consumption. Common brewers sold directly to local publicans. It was the Beerhouse Act of 1830, allowing anyone to brew and sell beer or cider on payment of an excise licence that resulted in a huge increase in the number of innkeepers lacking the skills and desire to brew. The increased demand for outside suppliers led to the gradual monopolisation of brewing into fewer and much larger companies. Hop growing peaked in 1885 when 5,930 acres were in cultivation.

It was the hop growers that used local clay to build the warm brick houses that replaced the old timber framed buildings. The splendid facades of the red brick, door-cased houses give the town its character. These were supplemented by the yellow brick, which arrived with the railway from 1848. The population almost doubled between 1801 and 1851 to about 9,000, when it was larger than Guildford, rising to 14,541 in 1901 and 38,000 in 2011. In 1853 an army camp was built at nearby Aldershot, which consequently grew from a village into a town, and this helped to support a large number of pubs in the town, several of which have survived.

Minding my mocha at Costa, I was greeted by an immaculately dressed attractive middle-aged woman with a broad smile. She had shoulder length blonde hair and eye-catching cleavage, not that I looked. She greeted me as if I was an old friend and sat in the seat next to mine. She began chatting away about how she needed her cappuccino. I had no idea who she was. I smiled back, not wishing to appear rude. She declared that Darwin was to blame for the idea that a husband should earn more than his wife. Logically, she said, the best wife should be a slave and there was no way that she was going to be ruled by such old-fashioned ideas. She was blessed by a thriving business, offering deluxe services, and worked her butt off to pay the mortgage. Being self-employed, she was happy to work long hours and pay for her son's school fees. He could go and roast himself. I asked her what school her son attended. I could barely get a word in edgeways. I managed to acknowledge that Winchester was a fine private school and stole a glance at my watch, which I hoped she saw. She caught her breath, imbibed and luxuriated in her moan. She kindly gave me directions to some historic buildings. I finished my mocha and bade her a good morning. She gave me her card and a wink. I unlocked my bicycle outside Costa and read her card. It was then that I realized that I had been chatting to the owner of an escort agency. I waved at her inside the shop and she waved back. At least some businesses in Farnham were booming despite the recession.

Looking back, I see this meeting as peculiarly English. It could have happened in a pub but it occurred in Costa. It is more socially acceptable to strike up a conversation with a complete stranger in a pub or coffee shop as opposed to a queue, at the garage or the doctor's surgery. The English suspend the normal rules of privacy and reserve to allow ourselves to overcome our habitual inhibitions at pubs and, increasingly now, at coffee shops. Englishness involves an unwritten code of conduct that exists regardless of class and ethnic origin. It can almost be said to have its own grammar of socially prescribed pleasantries, such as 'sorry,' 'thank you,' 'I beg your pardon' and so on. We even say sorry when it is not our fault! At times of extreme angst, the English use graffiti, which breaks the unwritten rules of Englishness. It is perhaps more English to moan than take action. I looked around for signs of graffiti. There were a few. I walked into the next street and saw a half torn poster for a gig flapping in the breeze and then a window poster:

In 1952 a woman knew her place
In 2012 she's still there

Farnham is well preserved thanks to a conservation policy adopted early in the twentieth century by property owners and builders. Subsequent restoration work has ensured the town's classical neo-Georgian style survives. Despite the throng of pedestrians I soon found the Old Hop Kiln, originally an oast house, next to the shopping centre and now an office block, The Hop Blossom pub, the 1619 almshouses in Castle Street and the Farnham Maltings, by the river, which has been the arts centre since 1968. It is all compact and with little lanes.

Close to the Maltings in Abbey Street is one of the most famous of English pubs, The William Cobbett, formerly the Jolly Farmer, renamed in the 1970s in honour of the radical writer, farmer and politician, who was born there. Cobbett (1762-1835) represents the caring, realist side of the English. He combines radical beliefs with conservative instincts. He has characteristics of mind that make him special. A combative self-educated figure, he agitated against injustices and gave voice to the inarticulate rural poor and achieved much that was practical and significant. Farnham justly acknowledges him. He is worth toasting at any of Farnham's pubs. There is a framed copy of his journal *The Political Register*, which he published from 1802-1835, at the William Cobbett. He also published Parliamentary debates, eventually taken over by Hansard and still published. When I was last at The William Cobbett I sampled a pint of Hop Head, a somewhat thin beer rich in hops, before being engaged by Original, a stronger dark beer with plenty of body and wondered if there was a connection between my taste for full-bodied beer and voluptuous women. On that occasion the bar was crowded and I was forced to find a way in by a professional woman sat on a stool at the end of the bar. It is against the code of Englishness to queue jump and even at a bar there is an invisible queue known to bar staff and customers alike. An Englishman or woman will always form an orderly queue of one. We do not have waiter service and so we go to the bar in an atmosphere of public haphazardness. I adopted a slightly anxious look and hopeful smile in order to inform the bar staff that I was waiting. I maintained eye contact but did not speak. The woman was bemoaning her boss. I instinctively made a supportive

98

comment. She did not respond and by this action told me that she did not wish to engage. Not being local, I was blanked. When my pint finally arrived I found a seat elsewhere. This is all part of the unwritten code of English behaviour.

Although exiled in America and France, Farnham is at the centre of his most famous work, *Rural Rides* (1830). Between 1821 and 1826 he travelled through southern England on horseback documenting the condition of villages, farms, farmers and their labourers. Reeling from War, the impact of land enclosure, threatened by revolution and struggling to adjust to population explosion the countryside appeared traumatised and so Cobbett rode to the heart of the countryside to report upon what he found. His incendiary journalism, written in farmhouses and inns brought the rural situation to Westminster. A mixture of invective and rustic vignette it is the best insight that we have of the condition of rural England at that time.

Incredibly self-motivated and a determined improver, Cobbett began his working life as a bird-scarer at Farnham Castle and ended as a farmer a few miles north of Farnham, ensuring that his labourers had the three Bs, bacon, bread and beer. He recounts the beginning of his education on a sand hill in a hop garden. It was at the top of this steep hill that he and his two brothers would take it in turns to withdraw their arms from their smock frock, lay down with their arms by their side and be rolled like a barrel or log down the hill by the other two. By the time they reached the bottom their hair, eyes, ears, nose and mouth would be full of loose sand and the others in monstrous laughter. This experience gave him the ability to become as he put it 'one of the greatest terrors, to the one of the greatest and most powerful bodies of knaves and fools.' He had his road to Damascus moment running away on foot to Kew Gardens aged eleven when he bought a copy of Swift's *Tale of a Tub* and walked back to Farnham awakened by the intoxication of words he did not fully understand. Trained to draft documents at Gray's Inn, he lost his job and became a soldier in New Brunswick, studying English grammar, teaching English to French refugees and compiling handbooks for his fellow infantrymen. Back in England, he clashed with his superior officers and tried to get them court martialed for profiteering from his men's food rations. They stitched him up and in March 1792 he was forced to flee to revolutionary France and from there, like that other great Radical, Tom Paine, he escaped to America. In time, he had to flee America after receiving a barrage of libel suits from republicans.

Back in England in 1810 he was imprisoned in Newgate for two years for opposing the use of flogging by the army. Once again he was forced back to America after attacking the Government for making peace with Napoleon. He returned to farm at Botley, planting 20,000 oak, elm and ash trees, and holding single-stick cricket matches. He was deeply affected by high land rents, rural poverty and the depopulation of villages. By the time of the 1819 Peterloo Massacre he had moved from being a Tory to being a leading Radical of the left. Measures to curb the Press had crippled the *Register*'s circulation and he was forced to sell his farm and move to London, which he loathed. It was then that he began his rural rides. He predicted and supported the Captain Swing riots of 1830-31 and successfully campaigned for the Reform Act (1832), one of the most important events in parliamentary history. The Act, although a series of compromises for Cobbett, saw the number of the electorate nearly double and representation for the industrial north. It began a process that was finally completed in 1948 when the country finally embraced democracy.

The music that I had heard for some minutes became more distinct. I turned a corner and saw an elderly man playing a one string bass. The string was threaded through an upturned oak beer barrel and tied to a metal stick. His hands were enormous and the sound so strong that I momentarily wondered whether he was a mime artist with a secreted iPod. His bass was an adaption of the washtub bass used in the Fifties skiffle groups. A piratical looking man was playing an accordion and a large elderly Teddy Boy, was playing piano. I half expected the police to arrive and stop them playing as this is Surrey and we do not allow such spontaneous septuagenarian outpourings. These were quality street musicians playing Zydeco and New Orleans boogie woogie. I rubbed my eyes as the strains of Professor Longhair echoed through the streets. I loved the simplicity and back to basics approach. Some of the passers-by looked askance whilst others admired their impeccable versions of 'Caldonia' and 'Crawfish Fiesta.' I began singing Dr. John's 'Right Place Wrong Time' as I continued my journey. Not long afterwards the wonderful sounds stopped.

Cobbett was a prolific writer. Amongst his other works that are still read *The Cottage Economy* (1822), a guide to self-sufficiency with information on brewing beer, making bread and animal husbandry, and *The English Gardener* (1829), which is still a detailed and surprisingly relevant handbook. It has some pithy asides, such as 'Purslane: A mischievous weed, eaten by Frenchmen and pigs when they can get nothing else.' When he had been in America in 1796 he had written some hostile comments about Thomas Paine, author of *Rights of Man*, (a work originally banned in England). After reading Paine's pamphlet *Agrarian Justice* he realized that he had attacked a defender of the landless poor. He sought to make amends and use Paine's fame for political reform and so in September 1819 he went to Paine's grave in New Rochelle dug up the body and sailed back to Liverpool with it. The digging up of the remains of famous poets and writers is not unusual. It happened to John Milton in 1790 and Lord Byron's tomb attracted so much gossip that in 1938 the Home Office gave permission for the vault to be opened. Whereupon the Reverend Canon T.G. Barker, very reverendly, lifted the damaged lid and found a perfectly embalmed Byron, with his clubfoot detached from his leg and at the bottom of the coffin. The local churchwarden noted that Byron's penis 'showed quite abnormal development.' Cobbett caused a sensation by being open about digging up Paine's remains. However, his efforts to build a public memorial to Paine proved impossible. The landlord of the Crown and Anchor in the Strand refused his booking and a hastily rearranged event in Fleet Street was cancelled when the King died and so it dragged on. Meanwhile Cobbett stored Paine's remains in his attic. Upon Cobbett's death what became of Paine's mortal remains became a Victorian obsession. It was believed that Cobbett's son sold off the remains in pieces and so Paine's skull went to Australia, his ribs to a Frenchwoman and a Bishop bought his right hand. What an irony that the man who first developed our theory of human rights should have his body bits scattered around the world? The reality wasn't quite so colourful. They were separated and passed through the hands of a Surrey farmer, a Guildford corn merchant, a London Quaker publisher and a series of radical activists, a Manhattan physician and Virginian Unitarian minister; all idealistic reformers involved with abolition of slavery, vegetarianism, women's rights and pacifism.

Farnham is blessed with many pubs their names synonymous with the town and The Hop Bag, Bird in Hand, Rose and Thistle, Holly Bush and Lamb that Thomas mentioned still exist a century later. Being a community focal point with a choice of ales and beers, which as Gerry Locklin's poem says, allows men to speak to one another, and the opportunity to relax, play games, dine on locally sourced food, in a friendly, dogs included, atmosphere marks out the surface of the English pub. Log fires and mulled wine in winter and a beer garden in the summer. Anthropologically speaking they are vital to Englishness as they provide a space for social bonding, allowing a looseness of conversation, disrupted by humour, and sociability. It is through the pub that we enact our egalitarian Englishness with laughter, wit and linguistic inventiveness. It should be like *Cheers,* the American comedy series, a place where everyone knows your name and you can chat to the bar staff and other regulars in a loose and comi-

103

tragic vein. Pub talk has its own rules and customs as does participating in a pub team, where each of the losing side must buy each of the winners a drink. Declining to follow the rules will certainly get your thrown out of the team and lead to social ostracism. The pub is vital to the social cohesion and integration of any community and it is where we learn the art of listening as well as speaking. Eavesdropping on pub talk can tell you more about your neighbour in two minutes than most conversations outside the pub.

The good news is that pubs are re-opening and have been closing down at a slower rate than five years ago despite the deepening recession. The current rate is about fifty closures per month. The great institution, idolised by Orwell, dominant in our television soaps, so loved by writers since Shakespeare's days, continues to adjust to competition by more clearly identifying their customers' needs and becoming a deeper part of a community. They have significantly lost the old spit and sawdust image as well as the distinction between the 'public' and more exclusive, 'lounge' rooms.
When I first started going to pubs this separation had a class undertow as well as a public and private split. Pubs are much more open-planned and classless now. Crucially they still have the public and private division in terms of distance from the bar, further away being more private and confidential.

I did not realize until I read Edward Thomas that some pubs provided books, as part of the 'home from home' experience, that had been handed down as part of the stock from landlord to landlord. In 1901 Thomas was decrying the inadequate provision of books in such pubs, although still finding books that interested him, and recalling that Shakespeare had spent a great deal of time in taverns. Free public lending libraries, following the Public Libraries Act of 1850, were increasingly replacing those inns that provided reading matter. By the end of the First World War, books were no longer part of the fabric of most pubs and inns. At my local, The White Horse, Stourpaine, the landlord, Chris Sargent began a book swap more than a year ago. It took off to the extent that Chris had to add extra bookshelves. The local book club uses the pub and customers enjoy a book with their pint or meal. Chris is keen on making his pub as good an experience as possible and is continually being inventive. This summer a theatre company performed an energetic and comic *Much Ado About Nothing* in the car park. He is as proud an Englishman as I know and sees the pub as a bastion of Englishness. Like a good actor, he knows his stage and how to pull the emotional threads of his customers.

Chapter Nine

The Oak

I decided to take a brief detour to Tilford to see Cobbett's oak and the village green as an epitome of the heart of England. Cycling down the heavily wooded Tilford road from the railway station I began to feel that I was entering a more familiar landscape. The presence of small woods, copses and hedgerows defined the landscape and left no doubt that I was in rural southern England. A wood pigeon flew by nose. They are the bane of the woodland cyclist. They are cumbersome and overloaded with ambition beyond their physique. Like jumbo jets, they have limited scope in changing their destination. I much prefer to cycle with a hawk or bat overhead. During the summer a bat will accompany me as I cycle home at dusk. They perform a dance, fly off and return, sometimes skimming my shoulder or head. I feel safe in their company, whereas pigeon produce a sense of consternation. According to Max Hooper the age of a hedge can be quickly gauged by counting the number of plant species in thirty yards multiplied by 110. Most hedges appeared between 1750 and 1850 as a result of the Enclosure acts and thus any hedge with ten or more species is likely to be very old, perhaps stemming from the Anglo-Saxon period. To quote Rilke, 'every step an arrival.' I felt as if my journey was tuning into something. The modern cyclist, unlike a walker, can travel quickly and I was beginning to feel tired of cycling and that I should walk again until I recalled George Bernard Shaw's walk along this road, with its heather verges, in the spring of 1888 to visit Henry and Kate Salt. He got drenched in heavy rain and bemoaned the uneven, ankle twisting roads and five hills. I had yet to encounter any hills. Salt, he wrote 'was a man of exceptional intelligence on most subjects ... country mad, and keeps a house at a hole called Tilford ... subsisting on the fungi of the neighbourhood and writing articles advocating that line of diet.' In 2012 it is still an idyllic place for a nature lover.

Tilford is widely spread out, centering upon a triangular green, where cricket has been played for almost two hundred years. This place is an artery through the heart of England. On 27 September 1822, Cobbett and his son stopped here to look at an oak tree, which had been a little tree when he was a boy and had become 'by far the finest tree' that he had ever seen. They measured the tree, which was in full growth and had a circumference of three hundred feet, with fifteen or sixteen limbs from the stem. It was, Cobbett noted, a pale leaf oak, standing upon a light loam with hard sandstone beneath, about one hundred and twenty feet away from and ten feet above the river's edge. The oak has great significance for Cobbett, symbolizing endurance and community. Note the attention he gives to the physical aspects and location of the tree. Apart from a little hole in one of the limbs there is no sign of decay. The veneration of the loam and sandstone is an appeal to love the core of the landscape. It is the soil and stone as much as anything that dictates what we can grow and build on the land. Not only that it is the chalk landscape and rivers that produce the springy grass that gave birth to our national sports, cricket, horse racing, angling and football. Cobbett sets his thinking on the soil within the context of historical time and growth. His sharp writing thus links the oak tree with the geology and history of the Downs with an appeal to English identity and personal roots.

The oak tree, as Cobbett knew well, was part of the fabric of village and rural living. Oak timber was used for shipbuilding and is still used for buildings and furniture. Its bark was used for tanning leather; the acorns for fattening pigs, its smaller branches and twigs are still used for firewood and charcoal making. Kindling wood is still important to the poorest inhabitants of a village today. One thousand year old oak logs have been found in peat bogs as hard and solid as ever. When I ran a country wine business I made oak leaf wine. As the must had a slightly antiseptic taste and weak bouquet I added fresh orange juice, a pot of earl grey tea, and a carton of grape juice to offset the medicinal taste and give it some body. It made an adequate dry white, sadly not as good or as profitable as silver birch wine. No wonder I went out of business. Oaks are attacked by gall wasps that hatch eggs secreting a fluid that stimulates the tree's defensive mechanism to produce knotty brown balls commonly seen during the winter. These oak apples have been celebrated as part of pagan nature worship for many centuries. Oak Apple Day was a public holiday commemorating the restoration of the monarchy from 1661 until 1859. Events celebrating oak apple day continue today in places such as Great Wishford in Wiltshire, where villagers gather in Grovely Wood and proceed to Salisbury, and many other villages around the country. At Great Wishford, mid thirteenth century rights to and within Grovely Wood, made into a charter in 1603, are re-asserted after a breakfast at the Royal Oak pub and a five mile procession to Salisbury Cathedral where they are proclaimed loudly and other traditional celebrations, such as maypole dancing, occur. In 1825 the Earl of Pembroke attempted to remove the rights and lost his legal battle. In 1892 seventy-four Great Wishford men formed the Oak Apple Club to defend the rights of the residents, subsequently joined by women and children each having distinct roles. There have been various disputes since then and so the celebrations continue with vigour.

Cobbett's Oak has its own mythology, as befitting a tree that is at least seven hundred years old. When the Bishop of Winchester ordered the tree to be felled for its timber the villagers filled it with hundreds of nails to prevent the foresters felling the giant. The Methodist preacher, John Wesley, is supposed to have preached by the tree and it was certainly large enough to hide a king but the King's Oak name stems from the tree being the largest in the wooded locality. The villagers took a sapling from the oak to commemorate the coronation of King Edward VII in 1902 and the Coronation Oak is thriving as far as I can see.

Sitting beside Cobbett's Oak, with its plaque on the seat, reflecting upon its survival and great age made me somber. It is now a slowly dying large stump held together by rusty metal sheets. I associate trees with the living and an interaction with the wind, birds and creatures. No one would be climbing this tree again. I tried to picture the vastness of this old tree in its prime to produce happier thoughts. The oak symbolizes endurance through all weathers and of striving forward whilst being centred in one place. I can relate to Cobbett's joy in seeing the Tilford Oak in that an oak marks and distinguishes a location, which when returning after a number of years provides comfort and represents a return to ones roots. I have these emotions when I see and walk by the oaks in the fields between Sturminster Newton and Fiddleford, where I grew up.

As the Barley Mow pub, dating from 1763, by the green was closed I cycled on in search of South Bank Cottage, formerly Gorse Cottage, where Henry and Kate Salt lived from 1884 to 1893. Like walking, cycling is a way of thinking and I wanted happier thoughts. Henry Salt (1851-1939), a junior classics master at Eton College, married Kate, the chaplain's daughter and moved here to live in a labourer's cottage, without servants, to grow vegetables and write. This move shocked their families and fellow Etonians, who had been worried about them since they began riding bicycles. Salt was a committed vegetarian, ethical socialist, pacifist, nature conservationist and man of letters. He founded the Humanitarian League, a forerunner of the League Against Cruel Sports, in 1891. Henry and Kate's brother, Jim, another Eton master, were part of the wide circle of thinkers, writers, artists and musicians that attended William Morris' meetings in Hammersmith. I must confess that I had never heard of the Salt until recently. Henry, though, was the first person to advocate animal rights as distinct from welfare in 1894. This significant epistemological break from previous thinking in *Animal Rights: Considered in Relation to Social Progress* was ahead of its time in acknowledging that animals have a distinctive individuality with a right to a life that should not be subordinate to human interests. Salts' *A Plea for Vegetarianism* (1886) and his *Life of Henry David Thoreau* (1890), provided Mahatma Gandhi, as he acknowledged, with the moral argument for his vegetarianism and faith in passive resistance. He wrote books on Shelley, Jefferies, Tennyson, James Thomson as well as wild flowers, the heart of socialism and the creed of kinship. He wasn't much of a nature writer, poet, translator and playwright and yet his devotion to finding better ways of living in the countryside is clear. He was a prototype of the peace-loving, alternative living beatniks and hippies of the post-1956 period. He provides an interesting contrast to Gilbert White, who lived at nearby Selborne and made significant contributions to the study of birds and gardening. White, who had no problem with shooting birds and animals, stayed in one village most of his life and is forever associated with Selborne. In contrast, Salt moved on from Tilford, was rootless and never wrote a book celebrating nature in one place. His writing was dispersed in essays and studies. White left us his journals where he continually recorded the natural year and his efforts as a gardener of flowers, vegetables, huge melon beds, homemade follies, wild flower patches and the ways he heated his greenhouses. White was in his way quite unorthodox and wrote a classic work in the development of our view of nature. Coleridge made notes all over his copy of *The Natural History of Selborne*, Darwin reckoned it was the reason he became a biologist and Virginia Woolf said that it left a door open through which we hear distant sounds. In essence, White offers a human engagement with nature. Salt never wrote a major work of nature writing that integrated his thinking. His work on Shelley is significant in that clearly establishes the poet's thinking on natural diet and ecology and it is now regarded as a forerunner of ecocriticism. He took readers through *Queen Mab* (1813), *A Vindication of Natural Diet* (1813) to *The Revolt of*

Islam (1818) and contributed to a fuller understanding of the poet's moral and philosophical position. It is from *Queen Mab* that the link between meat eating and 'All evil passions, and all vain belief, / Hatred, despair, and loathing in his mind, / The germs of misery,' is made and established as a justification for natural diet. He helped found the Shelley Society in 1886 with radicalism, feminism and vegetarianism at its core.

Salt was particularly successful in attacking the fur and feather trade. He coined the term 'murderous millinery.' It was out of the Fur, Fin and Feather Folk, women who refrained from wearing feathers in their hats, founded in 1889 at Croydon that the Royal Society for the Protection of Birds developed and ornithology grew in popularity. The Fur, Fin and Feather Folk took a pledge to 'refrain from wearing the feathers of any birds not killed for the purpose of food, the Ostrich only exempted,' the exemption rule being a fine example of Englishness. Gandhi met Salt and joined the London Vegetarian Society, many of whom were Fabians and Shelleyan, in 1889. It was through his reading of Shelley's *The Mask of Anarchy*, inspired by the Peterloo Massacre, that Gandhi's thinking on civil disobedience and passive resistance reached its maturity. Salt was an effective conduit of powerful ideas that are active today.

Salt attempted to live a simple life outside of the narrow conventions of respectable society according to the ideals of Shelley. Salt was a man seemingly prepared to accept all sexual attitudes and activities. He may have been inspired by Tolstoy's belief in sexual abstinence. However, his marriage to Kate was never consummated, as she did not want to be touched by a man. Kate, a spirited suffragette, musician and socialist, made a deep impression on Shaw and Carpenter, who became her 'Sunday husbands.' The platonic, intellectual companionship with Shaw flourished until 1898 when Charlotte Payne-Townsend replaced her as his unpaid secretary and became his wife. Shaw never consummated his marriage to Charlotte and dropped Kate entirely from his life. The Salt-Shaw friendship continued on a less intimate basis until Salt's death. Kate's relationships with Salt, Carpenter and Shaw provided the material background to *Candida* (1894), a play about what a woman desires from a husband. Interestingly, it is Candida that is responsible for her husband's success, a man with similar views to Carpenter. Kate's deep affection for Shaw grew and he was probably the only man that she might have had an emotional attachment with. Her love for Carpenter was more idealised and, of course, never likely to be consummated. She may have given Shaw the idea for the comedy of errors, *You Never Can Tell* (1897) and in particular the character of Gloria, a modern woman, working for women's rights, and with no interest in love or marriage. Despite having affairs with women, Kate stayed with Salt, living as 'friendly strangers' and providing the backbone to his life. She broke the convention of her class by working with her hands to clean and cook, no longer regarding manual labour as degrading but rather an engagement with life. She used her connections to support to the struggle against the slaughter of birds. However, it was her restless nature that led to their movement from one country cottage to another. Another close friend of the Salts was (Lord Olivier) Sydney Olivier, a Fabian civil servant and uncle of the actor, (Lord) Laurence Olivier. His four daughters were part of the Neo-Pagan circle of friends prominent in Cambridge and Bloomsbury with Rupert Brooke, Ka Cox, Darwin's granddaughter and Vaughan Williams second cousin, Gwen, Geoffrey Keynes, the Blake scholar who married Margaret Darwin, and Jacques Raverat. Olivier, who became Labour's Secretary of State for India wrote the introduction to *The Heart of Socialism* (1927) noting that Salt's humour and irony were perhaps too subtle for the general reader.

Salt, even more than Carpenter, is a forgotten figure that took an ethical view of living in the world and had faith in the Romantic imagination to create a new and better world. He had from all accounts a happy life that involved an animal friendly, simple and ecologically aware life. His humanitarianism and espousal of the ideas of Shelley, Thoreau and Jefferies contributed to thinking about alternative living and a reminder that simplicity and unorthodoxy have their own virtues. Salt, in essence, is the archetypal sandal wearing Other Man. His work against the slaughter of animals and birds provides a cultural context to Thomas' purpose in writing about the bird shop in Merton Road. Here 'linnets are rushing ceaselessly against the bars of six-inch cages, their bosoms ruffled and bloody' and goldfinches were making sounds out of place. A six inch long goldfish squirmed in a six inch diameter globe. It is here that the Other Man purchases a cock chaffinch in a paper bag and cycles towards Morden station releasing the fluttering bird near a garden. The symbolic freeing of the chaffinch is thus not simply the manifestation of Thomas' alter ego. He is associating himself, albeit at a distance, with the militant side of the animal and bird rights movement. The Salts were keen cyclists and part of the wider vegetarian cycling movement from the 1880's onwards. Indeed the Vegetarian Cycling Club began in south east London in 1887, becoming the Vegetarian Cycling Athletic Club in 1909. The Club was formed to prove that vegetarians could equal carnivores in ability and stamina in competition. The Club continues today. Thomas' Other Man is similarly by association suggesting that vegetarians have as much cycling stamina as anyone.

I couldn't find South Bank Cottage and cycled towards the Alice Holt Forest. As ever, my map reading was useless and I was using my sense of direction to find the right lane to cycle. Young Philip Marlow's litany, 'the oak and the beech and the ash and the elm,' came to mind as I whizzed past more trees. There are no elms, though. Alice Holt, ancient oak woodland, was enclosed in 1812. Conifers and pines, introduced in the second part of the nineteenth century, dominate and suck the wood of its old nature. The Forestry Commission acquired the wood in 1924 and it has effectively become a park with cycle ways and wide tracks and paths. The research station works on climate change, sustainable woodland management, evaluating woodland resources, biodiversity and protecting trees and was established in 1946. I found the solitary oak, George's Lonely Oak, named after a devoted forestry worker, that has become part of the cycling and walking experience of the forest.

Hunting forests, such as this one, were subject to harsh Forest law, imposed by the Normans, with punishments of castration and mutilation. Indeed the word 'forest' was originally a judicial term meaning land that had been placed off limits by royal decree. By the twelfth century there were 66 Royal Forests and 70 private chases controlled by strict Forest law. Here the King and other nobles had the right to keep deer, wild boar and other prey. 'Forest' also carries within it a meaning of being outside the public domain and it is this meaning that poets have utilised. Forests and woods are potentially where the world is turned upside down, as in Shakespeare's *As You Like It* or *A Midsummer's Night Dream*. It is a place of sexual discovery and assignation, danger and deceit, where pagan spirits can take over a man, such as Falstaff, as in *The Merry Wives of Windsor*. It is a fugitive world where lovers meet as in *Lady Chatterley's Lover*, a novel that I read as being as much about hidden aspects of being English and all its divisions as sexual love. In poetry from Shakespeare through Milton to John Clare, the wood is not merely a place of sanctuary, as in Andrew Marvell's *Upon Appleton House,* and testing of conflicting virtues and vices but also of potential regeneration. Deforestation has spoiled Alice Holt. It is devoid of wildness and lacks otherness. I hope that land is acquired for the oak to return. I have nothing against parkland like this. It is simply not an oak wood anymore.

I cycled through Buck Horns Oak, Blacknest and Binstead in an effort to re-align my journey with some of the lanes that Thomas meandered along towards Chawton and Arlesford. Like Thomas, I saw some rookeries but on ash rather beech. There was no sign of any gypsies around here or any part of my journey. The absence of gypsies and other wayfarers along the lanes is only something I realized after the journey.

Anglo-Romany Gypsies arrived in Hampshire to live in the forests, especially the New Forest, in the 1630s, having migrated originally from India through the Middle East to Egypt. Many worked in the hop fields, picked strawberries and did other seasonal work. Gypsies were outlawed in England until the second Egyptians Act (1783) and only recognized as an ethnic minority in the Race Relations Act of 1976. They have an almost hidden history and their strange upside down behaviour can be the source of humour for the English.

Gypsies started giving up their close to nature life, with its reliance upon herbal medicine and folk cures, in the early part of the twentieth century. In Thomas' period their brightly painted horse drawn wagons and carts made them stick out. Thomas, fascinated by their culture, noted their presence whenever he saw them. When I was a child they still wore bright colours, earrings, worked as smithies, made baskets and sold clothes pegs and lucky heather. They lived in or near woods, where they traded in horses, told fortunes, sold daffodils and went rabbiting. They cast spells both for and against the 'evil eye,' had a fear of cats and thought horses sacred. They decorated their Showman's living wagons and flat carts with gold leaf wheels, ornate ironwork, engraved mirrors and outside cooking box according to their wealth and status. Our understanding of this aspect of Gypsy culture was enriched by Jack Hargreaves on *Out Of Town, Country Ways* and his subsequent Channel Four series based on his own wagon travels. Since the decline in agricultural work in the late Sixties many have found alternative housing or moved onto permanent sites and work as landscape gardeners, motor trade workers and scrap metal dealers. As the gypsies gave up their decorated wagons they were often taken over by New Age Travellers that motorized them in the Eighties. In more recent time, some horse drawn wagons and carts have made a comeback.

In the late Eighties I was poet in residence at a school in Tadley, north Hampshire and was amazed to discover that the village had effectively started in the 1900s as a gypsy settlement on the common. The original village had been deserted sometime in seventeenth century. The gypsies had made their money from scrap metal in London in the Twenties and Thirties. The children and staff at the school were incredibly happy. Tadley, deficient in several amenities, seemed to be modern ribbon development out of the brush and heathland and had a distinct ambience. Tadley is the centre of besom broom industry, producing witches broom for the royal palaces. I stayed at the Fox and Hounds, a traditional pub owned by the gypsy family. I gave a reading in the lounge on my last night and sold several books and left a happy man.

There are still traditional families travelling through Hampshire and Dorset in search of seasonal work but their numbers are diminishing annually. Those that keep the traditional lifestyle are blander than their twentieth century ancestors and have a reputation for petty crime and horse stealing. They seem to be less rooted and living less off the natural world. They have fewer animals and are more anti-social and less reliable with beat up motor vehicles. Those that are semi-integrated now accrue social benefits and seemingly have a strict, albeit ambivalent moral code that allows them to steal but not offend. Their gender roles are heavily demarcated as millions have seen on Channel Four's documentary series *My Big Fat Gypsy Wedding* and their elaborate traditions for births and funerals are as ritualistic as ever. Others have adopted the dominant culture and carefully hide their background as they learn the idiosyncrasies of Englishness and attempt to live inside the law. Their extended family hierarchy, headed by the King and Queen, persists and for whom deference is a prerequisite. One partially integrated family member, from the Cooper family in the New Forest, drove sixty miles just to inform me that his mother had died. Unable to write, according to his behavior code, he was obliged to carry out his family wishes and inform me. Having delivered his news, he asked after my family's health, doffed his cap and was gone.

Chapter Ten

The Voice of English Summer

I arrived at New Arlesford just before six o'clock in overcast light. I quickly booked into The Swan Hotel, near the town centre, leaving my bicycle in the annexe and went in search of the Old Sun, the house where John Arlott (1914-1991) lived from 1961 to 1981. I strode like a man on a mission. The voice and poetic language of Arlott, commentating on Test Match cricket, is still the Voice of English Summer and acknowledged as representing the best of BBC broadcasting. He stands as a beacon not only of the articulate liberal radical tradition that harks back to Hazlitt but also widely regarded as the best of England. A humanitarian, who commanded respect, combatted hypocrisy, tyranny and converted opposition to his political vision, he had the ability to speak for the country. I walked from West Street, admiring the blues, greens and purple shop fronts in Broad Street and colour-washed houses of East Street. Half way along East Street I asked a lady locking a hair salon if she knew the Old Sun house. She looked askance. The Old Sun, a public house until the Fifties, was at the end of the town. By now somewhat disheveled I looked for the blue plaque, attached by the Cricket Society in June 2009, and was astounded by its absence. I walked away in anger. Arlesford is compact and has a laid back atmosphere. I felt comfortable there. I always regretted not meeting Arlott and this was as close as I was going to get. Those of my friends that had met him, such as the late Barry MacSweeney, spoke very highly of the breadth of his knowledge, generosity of spirit and sociable wit. I visited The Bell Inn, opposite the Swan, where Arlott imbibed with the Arlesford Historical and Literary Society and asked if anyone recalled Arlott. The barman raised his eyebrows and said that there was an old man likely to be around later in the week. My thoughts turned to Arlott's background.

Arlott was raised in the constricted cemetery lodge at South View, Basingstoke beside the Holy Ghost Chapel, chapel ruins and historic headstones. It is necessary to visit Arlott's birthplace and formative home in order to adequately guage the circumstances of his origins and have some grasp of his achievements. It is fleetingly seen from London bound trains at Basingstoke station and never ceases to jolt some phrase or memory of the man that commentated on Test cricket from 1948 until 1980. There is a public Arlott and a private Arlott that he chose, in the manner of Hardy, not to speak or write about. The closest we got to revelation was on the *Parkinson Show* interview when he read his poetry and was close to tears in recalling Dylan Thomas.

Arlott was a poet of place and literary broadcaster for the BBC, working with E.M. Forster, Dylan Thomas and Louis MacNeice. He inherited George Orwell's job at the BBC and become one of the greatest radio journalists of the last century on a par with Alistair Cooke and Richard Dimbleby. More than them, he became the personification of Englishness. Since Arlott's retirement, the only broadcast material that has come close to his impact has perhaps been Jimmy Perry and David Croft's *Dad's Army*, continually aired since 1968. With its evocation of England, represented by rolling hillside in its opening credits and a map, showing the threat from Hitler's forces and its nuanced reading of the class relations between Mainwaring and Wilson and the social structure of Walmington on Sea, *Dad's Army* has become timeless. It is *Dad's Army*'s reading and upholding of the rules of Englishness under threat that carries a powerful endorsement of England and the English. Arlott achieved the same impact with his voice and the power of his words, although significantly his radical liberalism has tended to be less prominent.

Arlott's ability to see two sides of an argument and seek a third way with some force of argument was forged at the BBC and in the pubs and clubs of Soho and Fitzrovia in the early Forties. Arlott succeeded George Orwell as literary producer for the BBC Eastern Service in 1945 and worked with E.M. Forster and several Asian intellectuals. He soon found himself working on other literary programmes, particularly with Dylan Thomas, Michael Ayrton, Louis MacNeice and bumping into the likes of Rayner Heppenstall, Geoffrey Grigson. Elizabeth Lutyens, Laurie Lee and Johnny Minton. He witnessed first-hand the extraordinary success of Thomas and the power of poetry. He came into contact with Neville Cardus at the *Manchester Guardian* and became a journalist. John Betjeman introduced him to poetry publishers and he was soon earning a living as a writer. His liberalism was nurtured, from his own account, by reading Montaigne's *Essays, Tristram Shandy*, Hazlitt, Shakespeare's Tragedies, the poetry of John Donne, John Clare and Andrew Young, Thomas Hardy, especially *The Woodlanders* and *Jude*, and John Stuart Mill. Arlott rented a room from Ayrton, adjacent to Broadcasting House, 4 All Souls Place. His first point of call was the BBC producer's pub, The George, at 55 Portland Place. This was a meeting place for composers, musicians, artists and actors. It was one of the central places for the bohemian quest for a spiritual and artistic reconstruction after the War. Arlott was in the thick of that creative cauldron. It was here that MacNeice and Roy Campbell famously came to blows in 1946. Alan Bush's *English Suite for String Orchestra* (1946), in particular, and Paul Nash's landscapes brilliantly capture the mood of that spiritual and political striving. Arlott's *Clausentum* (1946) collection, with Ayrton's lithographs, was part of that effort by poets, artist and composers to resurrect the forgotten parts of England, to re-connect with the English visionary tradition from Blake onwards, to return to the sources of Albion as a resource for rebuilding.

Soho provided the conduit for former members of ENSA, artists, poets, journalists, writers, composers, musicians and filmmakers to find work at the BBC, to network and argue over a pint or three. English comedic wordplay as exemplified by Ted Kavanagh's *ITMA*, Spike Milligan's *Goon Show* and Kenneth Horne's *A Much Binding In The Marsh* stemmed from Fitzrovia and Soho where surrealists mixed with actors and aspiring writers and producers. It was there that Dylan Thomas encouraged a young Marty Feldman to give up his trumpet and write more poetry and comedy. This creative and competitive scene gave Arlott the springboard to his own literary and broadcasting success.

I left the pub before it was too dark to see the pond. The

twelfth century pond constructed where the Alre and Itchen streams meet to provide fish for the Bishop of Winchester was celebrated by Wither in his poem 'Fair Virtue' (1622). It is the early pastoral poetry of Wither that inspired Thomas. He went to the lake to recite Wither's poem in praise to the goddess Thetis and land nymphs that provide the crowns of flowers and beech leaves. 'For pleasant was the pool, and near it then / Was neither rotten marsh nor boggy fen. / It was not overgrown with boist'rous sedge, / Nor grew there rudely along the edge / A bending willow nor a prickly bush, / Nor broad-leaf'd flag, nor reed, nor knotty rush; / But here, well order'd, was a grove of bowers: / There grass plots set around with flowers.' Thomas thus commemorated Wither's locality and the nymphs in an offering to the pond. He saw Wither as more of a poet of earth and water than Wordsworth and insists on the importance of visiting Wither's locality in order to 'taste something of the human experience and affection' that preceded the writing of the poem. Wither's earth has substance, he writes, whereas Wordsworth's is an 'insubstantial fairy place.'

Wither clearly meant a great deal to Thomas. He claims him as a local poet inseparable from his place. It is here that I saw the deeper connections between *In Pursuit of Spring* and the poems of place that Thomas wrote later. Thomas' journey is haunted, shifting, fleeting and tapping into the sources of regeneration. It is like his poems in that the reader senses something of a place and move towards an unsettling absence. His poems re-enact an absent presence in the form of a distance between the self and a dark place in free fall. This dislocation and state of collapse can only be filled by making a journey to the locality or by other restorative actions. The implication throughout is that village life should be strengthened. It is poetry of a peculiar action and underpins his literary vision of England. This vision subsequently chimed with the need to find the sources of Englishness and to revitalise England after the impact of the Second World War.

Thomas' appeal for literary travel was made at a time when railway companies were still urging travellers to see Wordsworth's Lake District and other literary localities. I walked towards the pond in sharp twilight and briefly saw the sluice gates from The Globe on the Lake pub garden before realising that I must eat and opting to return to the Swan. Walking along Broad Street I saw a plaque to Mary Russell Mitford (1787-1855), author of *Our Village* and one to the headquarters of the US Army's 47th Infantry Regiment stationed at the house from 1943 until D-Day.

Outside the air was muggy. I followed a Burrell Steam Engine around the side of the Swan to the railway station. The ten mile Watercress line connects New Arlesford to the national rail network at Alton. Originally saved from the Beeching cuts in 1966, it was closed by British Rail in 1973 and re-opened as a heritage line in 1985. The well preserved station has a considerable amount of rolling stock and is enthusiastically maintained. It was originally used to transport locally grown watercress to London markets. I noticed that it had a real ale evening train and a Sunday roast luncheon train as well as other themed outings to supplement a general and surprisingly cheap service. Essentially a voluntary organization, the Watercress Line appeared to be in good health and has hopes to eventually continue the line to Winchester. Had Arlott still been alive I could see him and John Betjeman involved in the push along the Itchen valley.

Watercress grows wild in the chalk streams and ditches around Arlesford. The industry grew with the advent of the railway, which could transport fresh cress to Covent Garden for the early morning market, in 1865. By 1925 cress was cultivated using regulated boreholes in gravel beds throughout the year. The industry, which went into decline in the Fifties and has lost 50% of sales in the last twenty years with supermarkets buying more Italian rocket is striving to make a comeback as a healthy food. It is full of vitamins and minerals and can be used in soups, sauces, pesto, scones and bread as well as salads. It helps to purify the blood and was grown as a medicinal plant by Hippocrates. Mechanical harvesters are now employed in what used to be a labour-intensive task. Arlesford has an annual watercress festival in May with a Watercress Queen. The town's pubs, coffee shops and restaurants compete for the best watercress dish and celebrity chefs, such as Antony Worrall Thompson and James Martin, appear to demonstrate the versatility of cress. I love watercress. It has a distinct vibrant and peppery taste. As a boy at Fiddleford in the Sixties, I picked wild watercress in a long ditch near a pond where I used to collect moorhen eggs and was captivated by its fresh tangy taste. The ditch and pond have gone but my taste for watercress remains.

At the Swan, I struck up a conversation with the waitress cum barmaid, a Goth in her twenties. She was happy with her life and a font of local knowledge. She told me about the local gangs and various subterranean snippets of local crime. She knew about the stained glass window memorial to George Wither at the Church of St Mary the Virgin, which Thomas did not see. Despite her local knowledge she hadn't a clue about Arlott. I told her some things.

By 1957 Arlott's cricket commentaries were so well loved that the BBC extended the cricket service to uninterrupted ball-by-ball coverage in a new programme. Test Match Special instantly became a cherished national institution with Arlott, Rex Alston, Ken Ablack (replaced by Alan Gibson in 1962), E.W. Swanton and former players, Freddie Brown and Norman Yardley providing summaries. The only interruption to the continual commentary is that other national institution the Shipping Forecast. When Gibson joined the team, Arlott had some genuine competition in terms of literary, classical and cricket erudition, wit and formal description. A former President of the Oxford Union, Gibson was also a poet, Nonconformist and Liberal. He became a drily humorous Marlowe to Arlott's Shakespeare until drink led to his dismissal from Test Match Special in 1975.

Arlott's cricket commentaries effortlessly drew listeners into a complex world through an enriching poetic language. His vocabulary was precise, pithy, modulated and centred on place in the here and now. He knew how to measure and beguile with his commentary. He was considerably more objective than contemporary commentators. To me, his Hampshire accent imbued the game with magic and a sense that it was open to all and not a privileged few. After listening to his commentaries one June day in 1966 I was hooked and became an avid listener and player from then on. I later discovered that Arlott had taken from Neville Cardus and C.L.R. James a thorough understanding of the historical, social and colonial background to cricket and was applying his knowledge to events as they unfolded on and off the field of play. His commentaries were part of my literary education as a child and contributed to my growing love of word play. I don't think it is too much of an exaggeration to say that Arlott contributed towards cricket becoming more of a national game in the post-war period. Everyone knew his voice and it became synonymous with those long, hot post-war summers. This is captured by Jack Rosenthal's 1982 television film, *P'tang Yang Kipperbang*, where the central character, Alan Duckworth's thoughts are voiced by Arlott in the form of a match commentary. Set in the late Forties, this coming of age story concerns Alan's attempt to have his first kiss with Ann and brilliantly evokes the impact of Arlott's voice.

Neville Cardus, writing for the liberal newspaper *Manchester Guardian*, illuminated cricket with imaginative description and elevated the art of cricket writing to literature by connecting sport to the outside world. He had a considerable impact upon Arlott's journalism and interests. It was through Cardus that Arlott read C.L.R. James, the Trinidadian Marxist, whose book, *Beyond a Boundary* (1963), poses the challenge (an echo of Kipling's question in the poem, 'English Flag') 'What do they know of cricket who only cricket know?' James uses this challenge as the basis for describing cricket in an historical and social context. He effectively showed how cricket meshed with his politics and understanding of class and race. As editor of *The Nation*, he successfully campaigned for the first black captain of the West Indies cricket team and changed the team's relationship with the public and paved the way for its success in the Sixties and Eighties.

Arlott adapted Cardus' literary approach making it more succinct for broadcast journalism. His exact and pithy words displayed deep understanding of the human condition and memorably evoked its epiphanies, such as a Clive Lloyd cover drive in 1975, described as 'the stroke of a man knocking the top of a thistle with a walking stick.' His distinctive Hampshire burr was also heard on *Any Questions?*, the BBC political forum, where his vociferous radical liberalism and humanitarianism brought rousing applause. He managed to impart a deep love of language to his audience, doubtless honed in countless drinking sessions with other Soho poets and habitués. He was also a hymn writer, wine connoisseur and book collector using his journalistic gifts to impart a deep love of humanity.

Social anthropologists and cultural commentators underline English social unease and restraint, locating its origins in the Victorian public school system. Arlott's outsider status made him acutely aware of the need for cold objectivity as well as subsequently giving him the scope to speak out. His passionate yet impartial commentaries gave him huge authority when he offered an opinion. He knew restraint and thus audiences trusted his voice. Topics of conversation that are taboo at dinner parties can perhaps only be aired in the pub, marital bed or law court. Privacy is something that the

English guard above all. It is like so much of Englishness an unwritten code and determined by rules. We have an unwritten constitution. Common law is built upon case law, essentially books of rules, teased, tested and appealed in court. It explains why our most cherished national games, cricket and football, are accompanied by enormous books of rules that are altered by committees. The English positively relish the uncertainty and anguish produced by suspect interpretation of written and unwritten rules. Suspect interpretations of our codes of behaviour invariably end up in court. As I write, the issue under scrutiny in the media is the boundaries of sensual massage and where exactly a masseur can go before it is inappropriate. This particular case rested on a woman becoming excited by a vigorous massage, accusing her masseur of abuse, and mistaking her physical arousal with an intention rather than an effect. Her case was thrown out and the masseur cleared of impropriety. The boundary of Englishness in manners is that sometimes blurred line between indifference and difference. Inappropriate touch is an entirely different business and one that is certainly private.

Arlott, like Betjeman, was recognised as quintessentially English. As true Englishmen, they guarded their privacy and past social involvements. Arlott's formative and creative years in and around Soho are glossed over in his autobiography, *Basingstoke Boy* (1989). One immediately wonders about his reasoning and what he did not want disclosed. Betjeman famously was interviewed saying that the biggest regret of his life was that he did not have more sex. Subsequent research uncovered rather more affairs of the heart than had been disclosed. The English love this subterranean world of secrecy and privacy and its subsequent controversial discovery.

Arlott and Betjeman's reading of Englishness as local attachment, as well as pubs and railways, is shown in the many anthologies of place that they edited and harks back to Jefferies and Hudson via Edward Thomas, Hardy and Housman. This though is only a partial reading. Arlott was passionate about human rights and dignity. He knew that the English, whether in Kent or Yorkshire, needed to treasure and defend their hard won freedoms from the Magna Carta, Habeas Corpus, trial by jury, freedom of satire, press, election and complaint. He was particularly trenchant against the militancy of Margaret Thatcher and the trade unions in the Eighties and was one of the few alternative voices heard during that period. Our attachments as a soldier or birdwatcher, banker or pigeon fancier are not so much to our country, much less government, but to our monarch (as long as they do as we wish) and ancient localities. We work by contract and demand that the rules of contract, whether written or not, are maintained. If a contract is broken we give the wrongdoer a chance to retract and then seek amends. This is the English way.

Arlott's most radical moment happened when Basil D'Oliveira, a Cape coloured player he had helped come to England to play cricket, was not selected on merit to tour South Africa in the winter of 1968. Arlott saw that 'Politics governs everything we do – the games we play, the way we play them, who we play.' Condemning the Test team selectors in press articles, he stated that he would not commentate on the summer South African 1970 tour unless the situation changed. This had a galvanizing impact that spread quickly through and outside the cricketing world. His uncompromising stance led a national debate about the tour and apartheid in South Africa. When Tom Cartwright had to drop out of the tour, D'Oliveira was selected as his replacement and the South Africans, suspected of collusion with the English selection committee, cancelled both tours. South Africa was then officially excluded from Test cricket until 1991 and the release of Nelson Mandela from imprisonment. Arlott's anti-apartheid stance may have stuck in the throats of the Tory old guard but his passionate belief in merit regardless of race or colour won the day and the anti-apartheid movement in England was given a massive boost. He seemed to me to speak for English moral justice and the wider world of humanity against apartheid.

After a breakfast of muesli, toast and marmalade, orange juice and coffee served by a different Goth, I began my ride towards Winchester. It was a sharp descent to the first traffic lights. A driver in a 4 x 4 impatiently and unnecessarily overtook me and braked sharply as the lights ahead changed forcing me to brake aggressively in order to avoid his vehicle. Had my brakes been worn I would have found it hard to avoid a collision. Luckily this was the only near accident on the whole journey. The driver sped away without a care. I took the right hand side road towards Itchen Stoke and Itchen Abbas along the way that Thomas cycled. I was soon regretting the decision. The lane was in a deplorable condition. I felt like I was cycling a 'boneshaker' and concentrated on finding the least worn path. To my right were beds of watercress with blackthorn in the background and the disused railway line beyond. It was a cold morning. The road was quiet apart from the blackbirds, sparrows and finches. Cock pheasants and pigs were visible in the fields. I looked for a leftward sign to the trout fishery in vain. There were more advertising signs and places of shelter in Thomas' time than mine. I saw plenty of blackthorn and then high above on a distant tree I saw some mistletoe. It was good to know that although the elms had gone from a century ago that the mistletoe and odd chestnut tree remained. After a few miles my fingers were raw and my arms felt as if I had been using a hedge trimmer for hours. It was a landscape devoid of cars and people until a speeding van hurtled past towards Winchester. My thoughts twisted and turned with the road. I had a sense of freedom on the wretched road. I felt young and alive. I thought of friends and loved ones near and far. The cold was numbing. I stopped after five miles for some water and to put on gloves. Just outside King's Worthy I joined the cycleway and saw a fellow cyclist ahead. It was a good feeling. I put on a spurt and was soon at their wheel. Other cyclists appeared and disappeared as we followed the road's camber. The signage was non-existent and so I opted to cycle on the pavement regardless. The sun appeared triumphantly as I orientated myself in the general direction of St. Giles's Hill and the Cathedral. I felt good.

Chapter Eleven

Winchester

Winchester, Anglo-Saxon capital of England in the ninth century, reeks of history. Here and there city workers, mums with babies and students emerged into the little sunlit lanes and onto the main thoroughfare as I made my way downhill towards the Cathedral. The grid of the streets were laid out a thousand years ago by Alfred, King of the West Saxons and developed from the remains of Roman occupation. It is easy to drift towards the Cathedral, chilling along the way as Winchester has an untroubled atmosphere. William the Conqueror commissioned the *Domesday Book*, compiled here in 1086, and the building of the Cathedral, one of the largest in Europe, dedicated in 1093. The Normans demolished the old Minster, dating from 642, which held St. Swithun and the mortuary chests of many Saxon Kings, in order to assert their dominion. That monumental figure, Bishop William of Wykeham developed most of its current structure. Wykeham established New College, Oxford in 1379 and Winchester College in 1394, which was intended as one of its feeding schools. King Henry VI replicated this model in the creation of King's College, Cambridge and Eton College. The four colleges have formal ties dating back to 1444. King Arthur's Round Table hangs in the Great Hall of the medieval Castle. The table dates from the thirteenth century and has been there since 1463. It was probably made for King Edward I who was present in 1286 at Glastonbury at the opening of the tombs believed to be those of Arthur and his wife, Guinevere. The earliest extant copy of Thomas Malory's

Morte d'Arthur was discovered at Winchester College library in 1934 and subsequently sold to finance College scholarships.

Guinevere brings to mind David Crosby's 1969 folk song of that name addressed to Guinevere by Lancelot from the *Crosby, Stills and Nash* album. Miles Davis recorded this freedom song as part of the *Bitches Brew* sessions in 1970. Graham Nash wrote 'Cathedral' here in 1977 after walking down the central aisle of the Cathedral and feeling a presence at his feet. He found that he was standing on the grave of Lt. Hugh Foulkes, a soldier, who died in 1799 aged 26 on Nash's birthdate. Nash recoiled and was moved to write the song against religious wars. Thomas Hardy proposed a liaison with the aristocratic and married, Florence Henniker, on the train from Eastleigh station to Winchester in 1893. Mrs Henniker opted for a visit to the Cathedral instead. They stayed overnight at the George Hotel and nothing happened. His disappointment is commemorated in the poem, 'At an Inn' and their relationship probably implied in 'A Broken Appointment.' Their intense friendship continued however and they wrote a story, 'The Spectre of the Real' (1893) together. A railway journey of comparable illicit intensity is echoed in A.S. Byatt's novel, *Possession* (1990).

Although novelist Jane Austen died at 8 College Street, beside the College Headmaster's residence, and is buried in the Cathedral, she did not have much connection with Winchester. She spent most of her life at Steventon, eight miles west of Basingstoke, at her father's rectory, and after his death, lived at Chawton, near Alton. Her last composition was a poem about Winchester, written three days before her death in 1817. Written on St. Swithun's Day, it is a tongue in cheek complaint about the locals spending the day at the Winchester races instead of their devotions.

Cycling and walking towards the High Street from St. Giles's Hill gives a sense of the geography of the city. The Cockney poet, John Keats stayed at Winchester between August and October 1819. He arrived from Shanklin, on the Isle of Wight, for the downland air, which he described as 'worth sixpence a pint,' having written prodigiously, nursed his dying brother and contracted tuberculosis. He was 24 years old and about to write his ode 'To Autumn,' one of the most enduringly popular and analysed of all English poems. It is perhaps comparable to William Blake's 'Tyger' in being open to endless speculation and critical desire. Keats wrote 'To Autumn,' in September at harvest time. It has a timeless quality, with its sensual imagery and fresh vocabulary and is rightly seen as an extraordinary embodiment of the English language.

From his letters to Fanny Brawne, family and friends we have a sense of the city, with its 'excessively maiden-like: the doorsteps always fresh from the flannel' side streets and 'collection of Lions' and Rams' heads', and where he walked. He wrote to his friend, the poet, John Hamilton Reynolds, 'How beautiful the season is now – How fine the air. A temperate sharpness about it ... I never lik'd the stubbled fields as much as now – Aye, better than the chilly green of spring. Somehow the stubble plain looks warm – in the same way as some pictures look warm – this struck me so much in my Sunday's walk that I composed upon it.' There is a useful book *An Historical Account of Winchester, With Descriptive Walks* (1818) written by Charles Ball that helps locate his walks. The Tourist Information has produced a leaflet that marks out a Keats Walk south from his lodgings north east of the Cathedral, past the College along the water meadows by the Itchen to St Cross Hospital and back again. I arrived at the Cathedral parked my bicycle by a bench and started to find the best vantage points to take some pictures for Louise. I stole quick peeks at the Antony Gormley statue, Sound II, in the crypt and the Pre-Raphaelite, Burne-Jones stained glass windows. One feels dwarfed and humbled by this imposing building.

Thomas had up to this point been following the old Roman road into Winchester. He now decided to cycle on a lesser road in the wrong direction towards Hursley instead a more direct route to Salisbury. I asked a woman in a black business suit sitting alone on a bench and looking sad the way to Hursley and to my relief she knew the way and gave me an animated outline of the way. I had soon forgotten half the directions as I had a growing need to find a public convenience and there were no signs of where I might find one. I cycled along College Street and was admiring the College playing fields when I saw an open gate and cycled in. A groundsman kindly opened the toilet by the Pavilion and provided directions to Hursley. This sent me towards the hospital of St Cross, the medieval almshouse dating from 1136, along the walk that Keats made. According to Simon Jenkins, it is the best preserved almshouse in Britain. It was here that the Bishop's son, Francis North as Warden from 1809, kept all the almshouse charity for himself after

137

providing for the brethren until finally exposed by *The Times* in December 1853. This Victorian scandal partly inspired Anthony Trollope's novel, *The Warden* (1855). I soon realized that I was going in the wrong direction and cycled back towards the warren of roads that bypass the city to the south-west.

Critics often neglect the local and historical context of 'To Autumn', trying to conflate the poem with the Peterloo Massacre, which agitated the hearts of all radicals. This ignores the fact that the poem is immersed in the figures of labour and idleness in autumn and a series of moments. It is surely much more about time and autumn than the meeting on St. Peter's Fields. I also think that the poem can be situated locally. Having cycled near the water meadows I can say that by squinting and removing all the cars and car parks there is still a strong sense of the natural world present. Local farming then was cyclical and based on sheep and corn. Sheep were moved from meadows in the autumn on to the 'stubble plains' to fertilise the soil in the spring. The 1815 Corn Law had produced high corn prices and an influx of soldiers returning from the Napoleonic Wars had lowered wages at a time when threshing machines were replacing labourers with flails. There was also some contention of what exactly constituted a corn bushel and middlemen were exploiting the differentials.

The Tourist leaflet ignores St. Giles's Hill and that is significant in the composition of 'To Autumn' as it would have afforded Keats panoramic views in all directions and of the whole city. St Giles's Hill had cornfields and looking south Keats would, I suggest, be able to see the City Mill, the granary in College Street and sheep in the water meadows beyond towards the Itchen. Similarly, he would have seen gleaners, barns, a walled orchard and stubble fields in the arable country to the north in the Abbott's Barton area.

However, in his letter to Fanny Keats on 29 August, he wrote: 'From the Hill at the eastern extremity you see a prospect of the Streets, and old Buildings mixed up with Trees. Then there are the most beautiful streams about I ever saw – full of Trout. There is the Foundation of St. Croix about a half a mile in the fields – a charity greatly abused.' This hill and view has to be from St Giles's Hill and offers sight of the Mill and granary. The socio-economic and geographical context, from St Giles's Hill south, offers a slant on the autumnal imagery. It is possible to read potential tension in the figures in the poem. It is clearly a poem of cyclical time reflecting upon labour and idleness, surplus and overflowing. It is at an angle from the composite tensions of local agriculture and, historically, prior to growing unrest among agricultural workers. It specifically offers a reading of a series of natural relationships to the cornfields, the 'hilly bourn' in Winchester. The 'o'er brimm'd' Summer of the first stanza is personified in the idle figures 'sitting careless on a granary floor' and 'drows'd with the fume of poppies' on a half reaped furrow and eager or drunken figure watching 'the last oozings' of the cyder press in stanza two. The narrative clearly shows pleasure in these figures. The phrase 'all its twined flowers' indicates unweeded corn and thus neglect. There is the potential reading here then of withdrawn labour with its implications of protests against the farmers, millers and middlemen. The narrator then looks forward to spring in the final stanza that is filled with joy and pain. A 'garden-croft' being a small fenced agricultural holding is more likely to be seen south of St Giles's Hill rather than north. Swallows gathering to migrate in autumn and return in the spring consolidate the temporal nature of the poem.

These images and figures set within a still centre hint at something underlying the intoxicated idleness. It is this something that readers feel. Autumn, ripe goddess, built on the interaction between humans, the sun and the natural world is pleasurably linked with idleness and drunkenness within a cyclical framework. The sheep that are on the 'hilly bourn' in spring are in the water meadows in autumn. It is the cyclical sequence of the poem that most chimes with Winchester farming and make it a peculiarly local poem.

Cycling in muggy weather thankfully upon pavements and around a bewildering series of poorly signed roundabouts I finally arrived at a tiny cluster of houses that constituted the village of Pitt. It seemed likely to have become smaller since Thomas cycled by. I could only make out four houses before I started cycling the biggest hill of my journey on one of the narrowest of roads. I know I have 24 gears but that hill was way beyond me in that sort of humidity. Stopping to walk was a perilous activity and so I persevered until I found a tiny inlet about halfway and stopped to drink and mop my brow. After ascending the peak it seemed like I cycled downhill for three miles towards Hursley. I had been thinking about the background to my sense of direction and recalled that Darwin's parents were particularly worried about their boy spending so much time walking in the fields near their home. It was there that Darwin first realized the interaction between the weather, landscape and animals and developed his own natural navigation. This interest continued throughout his travels and was one of the early foundation stones of his evolutionary thinking.

I tend to feel that this interaction is basic to anybody that spends a lot of time in the natural world as I did as a boy in and around Fiddleford, Piddles Wood and Sturminster Newton. Walking my dog, I watched her sniff, use her ears and leave traces of her presence. I soon became interested in tracking animals, identifying footprints, listening for unusual sounds and looking for signs of animal or human activity. Whenever the imminent prospect of rain came I learned to assess the quickest route to shelter or home. I could use the breeze to smell the difference between vaporous woodland and open land and thus find my way out of dense thickets. I knew north and south as visual aids rather than abstracts, and west and east in terms of the weather and sunrise. Ok, I failed my Duke of Edinburgh Bronze Award in the New Forest. Our troupe arrived two hours late, missed supper and I was boohooed for lacking basic map reading skills and ignoring the compass. There had been a tortuous interpretation of number and location. In the end, my argument for lateral thinking and smell won through and we arrived at the correct location. I remembered that we camped near a river and that night my friends Jed and Chris saw a bright star sized object move in the sky and to this day have no account for what they saw. I was used to remembering landmarks, fords, best footing, and gates and things overhead and found a compass

141

redundant. Whilst I could not relate map references to locations, I later developed an interest and use of maps as a visual guide. Maps, though, were not what I wanted. I wanted sensual experience from following a path to see what was there. Walking into the unknown has always excited me.

Flooding was a regular phenomenon. My father was the local water bailiff and in charge of operating the sluice gates that helped determine the volume of water released downstream. Water's interaction animates a landscape unearthing new situations. It is continually in flux. A pool or water trough so redolent of consciousness for the Romantic and neo-Romantic poets is never still. Similarly, rain fills the air with smells and sounds and moves soil downhill. Like most boys of my generation I soon had an affinity with mud and loved getting mucky. I once got sucked into quicksand half way across a pond and was rescued by a rope and tractor. The poem that I wrote about the experience was full of sensual succulence.

Scents are part of the memory and messaging service between plants, creatures and plants, plants and animals. Taste, as the poet, John Clare, articulated is joyous, from heaven and open to all living creatures. In the woods and fields with birds and animals, and in my mother's kitchen, I learned to explore the sensual world without conscious thought beyond verification and direction became a natural navigation. In short, I used wide-eyed focus and the senses to find my way and had an awareness of water and earth movements.

Woodland dominates the three miles to and through Ampfield, towards Romsey. The pubs that Thomas notes at Hursley and Ampfield have gone. Several lanes without signposts offered themselves as the westward route to Timsbury. I was forced to use my OS Map 132 and discovered that I was either in the crease of the fold or beyond the map's end. Like Thomas, I was further forward than I thought. A jogger pointed me to a large tree lined footpath adjacent to the road that he'd run down. It was here that I cycled by some of the most luxurious homes in Hampshire. They were spacious and incredibly well hidden. I subsequently read that Thomas had made the same mistake and doubled back along 'a gravelly soft road among many trees.' This was my first close contact with the original surface of the journey and I was unaware of its significance. In Thomas' time the path had woodmen's huts made from stout branches thatched with hazel. The woodmen had long gone and been replaced by some of the wealthiest citizens of Romsey and Winchester.

I found the unmarked Jermyns Lane and the tiny farmland lane westwards. The road was in good condition to Brook Farm. I had left the woodland behind and I was now in open country. To my surprise there was an ample cycleway on the road to Timsbury and a cyclist ahead. I felt a compulsion to race and join this lithe female cyclist. She took the road to Stonymarsh and I went on to the Bear and Ragged Staff, where I arrived well before opening time. The 'triangle of rushy turf' and walnut tree had gone and it seemed desolate. I took a pic on my iphone and crossed the road to take the left turn along the Monarch's Way, past the trout farm on the left, over the river Test and the railway crossing on the Salisbury to Romsey line. Immediately beyond the crossing I saw an old stone bridge and decided to stop by an inlet as it was secluded and I needed to pee. Between the twisted hazel growths I found a well camouflaged lake. The sun came out and I felt blessed as I observed the duck, moorhen and diving heron. Poor Thomas had arrived in a hailstorm and being unable to find accommodation at the Bear and Ragged Staff was on the way to the Mill Arms at Dunbridge when he gave in to the storm and took the train to Salisbury, returning to cycle on in the morning.

I climbed the old uphill Dunbridge Lane. It was narrow and the weather suddenly darkened as if the previous sunshine had been a rare glimpse of an old flame. As Dr. Johnson observed in 1758, 'when two Englishmen meet their first talk is of the weather' regardless of the fact that they already know the conditions. That still applies now and yet England has relatively temperate weather. It is simply cold and grey and this has produced a cold and grey population. It is part of our social unease, from centuries of segregation that we resort to a common device to communicate. The English have difficulty speaking to one another and Englishmen especially have difficulties speaking to Englishwomen. Weather talk is used as a greeting, an icebreaker and displacement subject in order to help us get along. After the Second World War when men returned to their homes the sales of garden sheds rocketed. There are still more garden sheds sold per head of the population than anywhere else in the world. We take segregation for granted and hide in weather talk. Our weather is distinctly colder and much more variable than in California or Italy. It combines with our hills, valleys, woods, rivers and coastline and history to produce elements of our character. Our weather comes from the Gulf Stream, the North Atlantic drift, wind-driven sea currents that produce, apart from during autumn, mostly calm south-westerly winds. Our post-Second World War weather has changed from predominantly cold winters and long hot summers throughout the country to a more regional pattern. The north west has cool summers, mild winters and heavy rain all the year; the northeast has cool summers, cold winters, steady rain all the year; the south east has warm summers, mild winters, light rain all the year, especially in the summer and the south west has warm summers, mild winters, heavy rain all year, especially in the winter. England in fact is a series of small microclimates due to the relationship between air and land mass and that is precisely what I encountered towards Lockerley, East Dean and West Grimstead. This is hilly, open farmland and I endured a hailstorm, squally showers, a short sharp downpour, humidity and sunny intervals within the space of an hour and a quarter's cycling. There being no adequate signage, I took a wrong turning and went up Dean Hill and down into West Grimstead. I was relieved to pause ascending Dean Hill to answer my phone and arrange a pub meeting with Jed on Saturday and surprise him at my progress.

By lunchtime I was approaching Alderbury disheveled and in need of a beer, food and rest. I found the Green Dragon slightly to the right of a small junction on Old Road by the village green. It is a fifteenth century 4-bay hall house and seemingly sunk into the earth as entrance to the front door is down some steps below ground level. The bars are tiny. I was greeted by the barmaid Lucy with a big smile and made to feel welcome. I consumed Lucy's recommended pint with gusto, ordered a ploughman's lunch and read a list of pub landlords from 1620 onwards on a plaque. I must have looked a sight when I arrived. Nevertheless Lucy was the perfect barmaid and we were soon chatting away like old friends about the pub and Salisbury. After land enclosure and technological developments, tenant farmers increasingly hired labourers on a casual basis for specific work. The social and financial gulf between farmers and labourers widened. Subsistent payments under the Poor Law were inconsistently paid or ignored by magistrates. Following bad harvests in 1828 and 1829, bread prices and unemployment rose sharply so that by the autumn of 1830 rural poverty combined with agitation against church tithes and the introduction of threshing machines led to the 'Captain Swing Riots.' They quickly spread from east Kent through Sussex, Surrey and Hampshire to Wiltshire and Dorset. Hayricks, tithe barns and workhouses were burned, threshing machines destroyed and threatening letters written to rich tenant farmers, magistrates and vicars by the fictitious 'Captain Swing.' Distressed craftsmen and farm labourers used the Green Dragon as their meeting place at Alderbury in November 1830. They had come from the area that I had just cycled and were met by local landowners, who sent for the Wiltshire Yeomanry. The rioters entered the pub and thus were caught and surrounded when the Yeomanry arrived to arrest the ringleaders and disperse the crowd.

As I finished my third pint, Lucy told me that Charles Dickens stayed at the pub in 1842 and based his description of the bandy-legged tailor leaving the Blue Dragon inn with its creaking sign in *Martin Chuzzlewit* (1843-44) on his stay and observation of a local tailor. I was grateful to her for the literary connection and subsequently discovered that Dickens had visited Salisbury and surrounding area. I wished Lucy a wonderful wedding, thanked her for her hospitality and cycled off towards Salisbury.

Chapter Twelve

Salisbury

Cycling along the hedged road from Alderbury in intermittent sunshine I felt that I was approaching a tributary along the heart of England. The Cathedral spire, inspiration to novelist William Golding, dominated the view ahead, as it did for Thomas. The Cathedral view from the water meadows painted by John Constable is often cited as one of England's best views. Salisbury is at the heart of English thinking about history, identity and the georgic with a vast literary history. The Chalke Valley History Festival, six days of history lectures, attended by 15,000 people a day, testifies to the strength of that concern. Salisbury's growth stems from its water supply. In 1668 Pepys noted that canals flowed through every street in the town in his *Diary*. The Norman cathedral at Old Sarum was replaced here due to its streams and rivers. Neighbouring Wilton, the home of the Earl of Pembroke, was eclipsed by Salisbury when the river Avon was forded at Harnham, diverting traffic away from Wilton into Salisbury. The Cathedral's Chapter House holds one of the original copies of the Magna Carta from 1215. It is the peculiar confluence of rivers, woodland, farming and thoughts of liberty that have inspired the English to value their independence, ancient monuments and, when necessary, to protest and survive. That local tradition from the Sidney-Spenser circle (that met at Wilton House), Michael Drayton's *Poly-Olbion* (1612), through Hazlitt, Wordsworth, Cobbett, the Captain Swing rioters, E. M. Forster, Edward Thomas, Thomas Hardy, John Arlott and so on is alive and well. Its most recent example is Jez Butterworth's *Jerusalem* (2009), a play that scuffs against idealized and sanitized versions of rural England and defends the defiant and wild side of Englishness. Salisbury and surrounding villages are less congenial than thirty or forty years ago. It is a troubled area with an edgy, rundown feel.

Set somewhere near Salisbury in rural Wiltshire on St. George's Day, the morning of a country fair, the play is full of allusions to England, literary, mythological and historical references. Kennet and Avon Council officials serve notice to evict a Gypsy, Johnny 'Rooster' Byron, and his caravan from a wood. 'Rooster' Byron is a wanted man. His son wants him to take him to Flintock Fair, his dysfunctional friends want his ample supply of drugs and alcohol and Troy Whitworth wants to give him a serious kicking. The hobbling figure of Byron, his name recalling a poet that was 'mad, bad and dangerous to know,' has resonances of Robin Hood, Puck, John Barleycorn, the Green Man and St George against the Dragon. Cycling from the Green Dragon, this heritage and texture was not lost. Indeed, the play emblazons its setting with a texture that echoes Shakespeare. It is a rip-roaring comedy with the reek of authenticity and uplifting, fabulous, incantatory language. Rooster, a cocky island of a man, is a lord of misrule, with teenage girls emerging bug-eyed and doped-up from behind his sofa, and a shielder of youth from more ferocious predators. He is endearingly hopeful, eloquent and comic in the face of encroaching bureaucracy and public order acts. Like England, his empire is depleted and he is a shadow of his former self and doomed to be slain by the dragon of officialdom.

Its localized, drink and drug addled comedy, 'I leave Wiltshire, my ears pop,' is mixed with malevolence from the new estate with its vindictive petition against Rooster. The play's title, derived from William Blake's 1808 poem, its cultural accretions embody England through its 'green and pleasant land' and the belief that the English are God's chosen people. The play shows the Council, Salisbury Magistrates Court, the Rotary Club and the new estate against 'the unwashed, unstable, unhinged, friendless, penniless baffled beserkers' of Flintock and revels in the joys of local community through its energetic fun. It is in the tradition of the local defence of liberty, with all its attendant difficulties implied.

With the sun coming out again, I cycled over New Bridge and when the traffic allowed walked over the wide road to slip down into the old outer road towards the south gate of the Cathedral. Here I crossed over Harnham Bridge, 'where the tiled roofs are so mossy, and went up under that bank of sombre-shimmering ivy' in Thomas' footsteps having taken some pictures. It is still as he described. When Thomas arrived in Salisbury on a Sunday morning he noted that there were more birds than people and that the streets, devoid of shoppers, were cold and naked. He lists the succulent names of the inns, such as, Round of Beef, Ox and the Haunch of Venison, a pub that used to be a eighteenth century brothel for the Deanery, reached from a path at the back of the Church of St. Thomas, and still has its original waiting rooms.

Thomas' idea of cycling through southern England pointing out its geography, weather, history and literary heritage derives from Drayton's attempt to preserve England's history through topography and forge a national identity. This included written itineraries and routes across a territory with particular histories, points of interest and local lore. The controlling image of the river stems from Edmund Spenser's *Prothalamion* (1596). This idea and image fuels *Poly-Olbion*'s celebration of national diversity, with rivers, as loci of conflict and song, serving to unify the country. The final part of Book One ends with a celebration of Kentish independence and liberty against Norman law. Wordsworth echoes this in 'To the Men of Kent,' one of the 'Sonnets dedicated to Liberty,' in *Poems* (1807). 'Ye, of yore / Did from the Norman win a gallant wreath; / confirm'd the charters that were yours before.' This patriotism is rooted in the tradition of local defence of liberty that Butterworth's *Jerusalem* echoes so gloriously.

I cycled on the West Walk path between the Salisbury Museum, Medieval Hall, Wren House and the Cathedral on the right towards the Close. I passed the home of Ted Heath, the former Prime Minister, with its queues of tourists waiting to visit and on to North Walk, with the rooms where Golding taught on the right and where Handel played his first concert in England above the far right exit into St John Street. I walked down the High Street and took the first left along Crane Bridge Road and into Mill Road towards the water meadows.

In November 1830 the Captain Swing riots spread throughout the Salisbury area and lasted for six weeks. Local agricultural workers were amongst the lowest paid in England

and risked their lives and imprisonment to improve their lot. The painter, John Constable was not immune to what was happening and if you compare his *Salisbury Cathedral From The River* (1820), which shows the landscape as a social playground, with *Salisbury Cathedral From The Meadow* (1831), you will see the stark contrast. What is amazing is that the exact spot where Constable painted one of his most literary and symbolic works is still in the water meadows on the path to Harnham and when you stand there the painting becomes more explicable and that was my destination.

Constable portrays two agricultural labourers crossing a stream by horse and cart set against Salisbury Cathedral under a rainbow, after a storm, and next to an outsized ash tree on the left, moving towards a shrivelled ash to the right. In the central foreground is a dog, with a grave to the left and fencing to the right. The ash trees are symbolic of life's disparities, with the Cathedral representing faith and resurrection and the rainbow hope. The rainbow has to be symbolic as it is in the wrong meteorological place. The dog appears to be observing the scene and directing the viewer's gaze toward the horse and cart, which is empty. They could have delivered grain to the city or come from the city without grain.

Conventionally read the painting is dominated on the left by the shrub and gigantic ash tree soaring above the distant Cathedral and the illuminated eye of the storm in the mid-central and upper part of the scene. The bright light is at a distance beyond the spire. The rainbow encloses the darker half of the painting that is mirrored by the circling stream, representing consciousness and the enduring faith of the labourers in balance with the natural world during an economic and political storm. It is thus an emotional response, with the rainbow of hope encompassing faith and the labourers in harmony with the wildness of the natural world, to the social-political situation. However, when you stand at the exact place that Constable chose and widen the frame of reference you see to the left beyond the Church of St Thomas is Fisherton Mill, where grain was used for bread making and that to the right leads to the older water-mill at Harnham, where grain was used for bread-making and stock feeding. We are thus at the centre of the city's agricultural economy and its supporting relationship to the neighbouring villages. The painting is thus built around an absence of the exact economic conditions that mark the empty cart.

The painting has a nine-line quotation from James Thomson's *The Seasons* (1726-30). *The Seasons* was a celebration of the divine order behind the apparent chaos of nature. For the Romantics, including Constable, it was memorable for its descriptions of the weather, landscapes, of the moods and colours of the natural world. Mood is dominating economic relations in this painting. Looking again, the dog, separated from the labourers by the stream and on the wrong side to be part of their company, centres the non-economic human connection with the land and acts as a psychological bulwark against wrenching economic conditions.

Constable's Cathedral iconic view serves to show how economic relations, poverty and the struggles behind them are blanked out of cultural memory. It is a failure to appreciate local history and distinctiveness.

I stood on the spot where Constable painted, as I have done before, and felt that tinge of awe. To my left I could cycle along Thomas' route to St Andrew's Church at Bemerton, where the poet, George Herbert was rector and died in 1633. No longer a separate village, Bemerton is one of the poorer parts of Salisbury. St Andrew's is a chilly, tiny Low Anglican church, with a strong atmosphere of piety, a stained glass portrait of Herbert, and palpable sense of connection to the poet. It was here Thomas recalled Herbert's sonnet on Sin. When I looked at the altar in St Andrew's I felt the intense drama of Herbert's *Temple* poems come alive, especially in 'The Collar' with its startling opening, 'I struck the board, and cry'd, No more / I will abroad' and recalled him being found by a local prostrate before the altar. His emotional struggles towards a deeper faith echoed. Humbled by its simplicity, I left with a desire to return to the poetry and the building.

I could cycle north west to Salisbury Plain, where Wordsworth walked in August 1793, an experience that produced *The Salisbury Plain Poems* (Cornell 1975), 'The Female Vagrant' first published in *Lyrical Ballads* (1798), and fed into *The Prelude*. He changed these poems several times. The unpublished *Adventures on Salisbury Plain* (1795), a dark gothic poem concerns a sailor who, having been press ganged into the navy after war service, becomes a murderer and robber to provide for his family. Penniless and an outlaw, he meets a soldier's widow as he walks across the Plain. She is homeless, penniless and has lost her family. Both are outcasts and face the inhumanity of the law. The poem relentlessly shows the human impact of war and links human waste to the historical landscape. This poem was later revised as *Guilt and Sorrow: or Incidents upon Salisbury Plain* (1842) with the image of the sailor's suicide 'hung high in iron case' removed. This self-censoring of the younger, radical Wordsworth shows how the struggles of the rural poor and outcasts can be written out of memory. By contrast, W.H. Hudson in his cycle journey (*A Shepherd's Life* 1910) across the Plain writes about a young boy, a bird-scarer, running across the ploughed field towards the road merely to see him pass and neutralises rural labour by avoiding any polemical, ecological or contemplative input. Hudson's non-committal tones and registers, omitting the rawness of the georgic, caught the Edwardian mood of nostalgia for rural ways and were immensely popular. Bird scaring did not die out in the area until the Thirties.

I could cycle north and east a few miles along the A30 to Figsbury Rings, the Iron Age hillfort, where E.M.Forster had some experiences that fuelled his novel, *The Longest Journey* (1907). It was here that Forster met a lame shepherd boy in September 1904 who taught him to look at the landscape until as he wrote, 'it began to look back at me.' The meeting transformed and fired the way Forster saw the natural world and human relations and England. His character, Rickie, sees Salisbury, its converging water, the Plain, its chalk streams, Old Sarum and woods as 'the heart of our island.' Rickie eulogises on the chalk landscape declaring, 'The fibres of England unite in Wiltshire'…'we should erect our national shrine.'

155

Forster's symbolic and philosophical novel contrasts the local waterways and 'slowly modulating' chalk downs with the quadrangular academic world of Cambridge. It shows the public school, Cambridge version of England, with all its class exclusivity, lacking the closeness of a fuller, emotional and rooted life. Rickie, 'the lonely and deformed' character, recites lines from Percy Shelley's *Epipsychidion* (1821) at Figsbury Rings that establish the novel's theme and gives it its title. 'I was never attached to that great sect / Whose doctrine is that each one should select' one mistress or friend and leave the rest 'To cold oblivion' and 'The dreariest and longest journey.' The recitation reinforces the significance of the ancient location and imbues the novel with a sense of deep roots.

The narrator sees Salisbury as a living creature with powers of movement, and 'ugly cataracts of brick' looking 'outwards at a pagan entrenchment' and away from the Cathedral, neglecting 'the poise of the earth, and the sentiments she has decreed.' 'They are the modern spirit,' he observes. He goes on in an unconscious echo of Drayton, although possibly not of Wordsworth. 'Streams do divide. Distances do still exist. It is easier to know men in your valley than those who live in the next. It is easier to know men well. The country is not paradise (an embedded reference to both Sidney's *Arcadia* and Milton) and can show the vices that grieve a good man everywhere. But there is room and leisure.' Forster's sense of national identity is defined like Wordsworth by topography and regionalism in the tradition of Drayton and Camden's *Britannia*.

A little way beyond Figsbury Rings is the village of Winterslow, where an extraordinary man lived, wrote and painted for the best part of twenty years between 1808 and 1828. He stalked the fields, woods and Cathedral and yet there is no sign left of this colossus in the city or at Winterslow. He is not studied at many English Universities or at English schools and his work is out of print and those that do want to read him need to haunt second hand bookshops. William Hazlitt (1778-1830) was a master of English prose, a beautifully modulated essayist, the first great theatre and art critic, a political journalist in the manner of Cobbett and incredibly, he was a philosopher and literary critic, recognising the talents of Coleridge, Wordsworth, Keats and Charles Lamb. He interweaves literary quotations in order to reinforce points in his essays and was a tremendous dinner guest, full of eloquence, wit and imaginative argument. His *Table Talk, or original essays* (1822) serves as a handy introduction to his brilliance. A man of great honesty, he struggled to make a living from his painting and journalism and was always vehement in thought regardless of fortune. He is considered one of our greatest essayists and admired for the sheer joy and exuberance of his writing style. The big thing about Hazlitt is that his writing is as fresh and thought provoking as ever. It is literary and conversational. Of all the writers that affirmed English liberty along this journey, Hazlitt is the most profound and yet he has disappeared from our culture the most. I think of MacGilchrist's analysis of the malaise. It is to the shame of our national culture and confirms the dominance of mechanistic over humanist thinking. Meeting a fan of Hazlitt is like belonging to a secret society of English free thinkers. They come from across the political spectrum, recognizing his eloquence, sharp wit, love of oratory, and belief in the English popular will. His admiration of Napoleon Bonaparte is something that the English have never really understood. He is as profound a thinker as Kant and Hegel and yet capable of writing in a personal and inviting manner. In 'On Going A Journey,' he writes 'The soul of a journey is liberty, perfect liberty, to think, feel, do just as one pleases. We go a journey to be free of all impediments and of all inconveniences; to leave ourselves behind, much more to get rid of others. It is because I want a little breathing-space to muse on indifferent matters, where Contemplation,

'May plume her feathers and let grow her wings,
    That in the various bustle of resort
Were all too ruffled, and sometimes impair'd'

that I absent myself from the town for awhile, without feeling at a loss the moment I am left by myself.' It is passages like that that I never tire of and his writing is full of them. Read Hazlitt aloud and you will sense his poetry. Contemporary critics praise a lot of turgid prose. Hazlitt was an uplifting writer who knew what he wanted to say and wrote as clearly, sensually and forcefully as possible. He praised Wordsworth, Coleridge and Southey and gave them a hard time when they lost their radicalism. He dismissed Coleridge as a 'sleep-walker, the dreamer, the sophist, the word-hunter, the craver after sympathy' and wanted more indignation against tyrants, sycophants and servile sophistry.

Hazlitt gave Thomas a sense of the journey as dissent and essays such as 'On My First Acquaintance with Poets' show the links between walking and writing, reading and journey, landscape, people and writing. He was the primer for deeper awareness. In October 1817 Hazlitt stayed at the Winterslow Hut, now the Pheasant Hotel, and wrote,

'My style' …'flows like a river and overspreads its banks. I have not to seek for thoughts or hunt for images: they come out of themselves, I inhale them with the breeze, and the silent groves are vocal with a thousand recollections:

> And visions, as poetic eyes avow
> Hang on each leaf and cling to every bough…'

I cycled on to Salisbury Railway Station and took the south west train to Gillingham. I sat with a young woman in an outer carriage area. She was unemployed, reliant upon public transport and desperate. I suggested that she looked into the possibilities of loaning a bicycle to help her situation and explain to potential employers the difficulties of not having a car in a rural area. She didn't like the prospect of cycling the hills. I told her about the various 'Cycle to Work' schemes, the growing number of cycleways and number of people using the trailway. In the end, she smiled and said that somehow she would find a bicycle if only to keep fit.

From Gillingham Station I cycled the nine miles to Sturminster Newton in wonderful sunlight. Elation began to overcome tiredness as I passed through East Stour, where the novelists, Henry and Sarah Fielding grew up in the early eighteenth century. Henry's courting in Lyme Regis in 1725 went into his comic novel, *Tom Jones* (1749). Sarah's novels and criticism have recently been re-discovered. It is a hilly ride and I was relieved to go through Marnhull, the setting for Tess's cottage and the Pure Drop Inn, in Hardy's *Tess of the D'Ubervilles*, and downhill towards Hinton St Mary. I passed my maternal great aunt Bessie's cottage on the right and the cricket pitch on the left. With growing excitement I freewheeled downhill into Sturminster, described by the late Paul Hart as the centre of the world and where Hardy lived for a year. I looked at my old school playing fields on the left. It was there that I first listened to John Arlott and Alan Gibson on Test Match Special in 1966 commentate on the series against India. It was there that Paul filmed me running to illustrate my poor style. It was there that Jed and I forged an unbroken eighth wicket stand of sixty runs for the School team to beat the Parents XI in July 1969. It was there that I learned to continue and not give up. I thought of all my old school friends that had died young. I thought of how their loss had given me a sense of responsibility to work hard and honour their memory and the place that we all loved. I thought of the 900 year old cattle market now reborn through the Exchange community and arts centre. I thought of Yasar at the Poets Café and his selfless help for others. I thought of Paul's cousin, Phil, and his extraordinary shop. I passed Harry Dawe's home and garden on my right and the old town workhouse on my left. My elation was palpable. In brilliant sunshine, I felt that I was coming home. I was soon climbing the steps to my parent's home and given the best welcome that I could have hoped for.

About the Author

David Caddy is a poet, essayist, critic, literary sociologist and historian. He lives and works in rural Dorset from where he has edited the international literary journal *Tears in the Fence* since 1984. His most recent books are a collection of belles-lettres, *So Here We Are* (Shearsman 2012) and a book of poetry, *The Bunny Poems* (Shearsman 2011). He regularly publishes essays and criticism on literary and cultural matters. He was co-author of *London: City of Words* (2006), a literary companion, with Westrow Cooper and directed the Wessex Poetry Festival from 1995-2002 and the Tears in the Fence Festival from 2003-2005.

Made in the USA
Charleston, SC
17 June 2013